Funny Man Down

Selected Columns from McCune's Manchester

by Adam McCune

Charles Trott Publishing
Published by Charles Trott Publishing, 36 Libbey St, Manchester, NH, 03102

Printed in the USA

First Printing, October 2010

Library of Congress Control Number: 2010937843

McCune, Adam 1978-

     Funny Man Down, Selected columns from McCune's Manchester / Adam
     McCune (First Edition)
       p. cm.
     ISBN 978-0-6154070-2-9 (trade pbk.)

Cover design by Adam McCune
Cover photo by Christopher Gentry

For Broden and Isak

Contents

Family

The Unemployment Chronicles

How to Read this Book

Instructions? Well, yeah...kind of.

This book is comprised of selected columns that appeared in McCune's Manchester, in the metro section (and occasionally the front page) of the New Hampshire Union Leader.

Each column is printed in its entirety. Occasionally preceding the column is a short introduction. It's in these introductions that the back stories and behind the scenes elements are told. A few comments from readers are also included here, as I tried to make this book as interactive as I could.

After these introductions, the words "McCune's Manchester" and the date of the publication appears, followed by the column itself.

Relax, kick back, and enjoy!

AdamMcCune.com
Facebook.com/adamjmccune

Funny Man Down

by Adam McCune

Introduction

I gave my parents grief. I'm not going to say I was a brat, but my mouth never stopped moving when I was young. Maybe you could say I was a little "mouthy" in those days. That would be fair. I always thought my voice was louder and easier to pick out of a crowd. That usually resulted in me spending more time in trouble for talking than anything else. Every report card I received from Kindergarten to graduation said something along the lines of "Adam is a good student, but has a habit of talking too much."

What can I say? I've always liked to tell a story, no matter how small my audience was at the time.

Honestly, some of my first fans were those same teachers. My second grade teacher, Mrs. Erickson, was amazed at how many things she heard from me before anyone else, even the news. She told my mother this during parent-teacher conferences.

"Adam told me last week that there was talk about going to an eight day week," she told my mother. "Well I thought it was foolishness and laughed it off. Wouldn't you know, I heard it on the radio this morning?"

My mother probably nodded her head at this point, she was used to my constant talking and storytelling. I'm still not sure if she was listening intently or just became really good at blocking me out. Either way, she was my first fan.

I have a distinct memory of following her around while she did chores around the house. She would be folding clothes and I would be going on and on about something that happened in school.

While my mother would prepare dinner, I would be retelling some story I heard on the news. When she would get tired of hearing me, I would talk for hours into a tape recorder and pretend I was Chuck Knapp on

KS95, a radio station out of Minneapolis, Minnesota.

There is a tape of me, I'm about five years old, introducing songs and telling jokes. My mother found it a few years ago, and I don't think I recognized what it was. It was the beginning. I was laying the groundwork for something and had no idea that I was doing it.

By the time I graduated high school, I was sure I was headed for a life-long career in radio. I went to a tech school that taught me some basics and waited a few months before I landed that first job.

I was terrible. Awful. And I knew it. Those first few months were painful. I wanted to quit. My boss was a tyrant, a mean old curmudgeon, and one of the worst individuals I had ever met. He was running a Christian radio station in Wisconsin, not far from where I grew up. At night, I would sit in my tiny apartment above a bar in the town and slap away at a typewriter I had "borrowed" from work. I didn't have cable, there was no television reception, and I knew how awful the radio station was, so entertainment was sparse.

So I typed. I typed up silly stories like "Why People Suck at Driving in the Winter", and long diatribes about everything that was going on in my head. I didn't know it, but it was the start of my writing.

When I finally handed the keys to the radio station to that mean old man one night and said "I won't let you ruin my radio career," I felt great. The first thing they taught me in radio school was to never walk out of a job. The second thing they taught me was to spend a year at your first radio job, no matter how bad it was.

Well, I couldn't do it, and yet, I knew quitting three months in was the right move to make. I had no other job, I was moving back in with my parents, and yet, it felt wonderful.

Soon, I landed a new job that eventually turned into a morning gig at another station. I would spend all day at the station, sometimes spending hours writing and producing comedy bits. All the while, I was telling a story.

I moved up, first to management, then to a bigger, competing station. All the while, I thought this was it for me. Radio was my life.

When I moved to New Hampshire, it was this same radio career that was the catalyst. I was growing tired of my home state. My new family and I needed a change of scenery, and I honestly thought that was going to be somewhere like Minneapolis or Madison or Milwaukee. One of those demo CDs from that desperation made its way to New Hampshire where Bob Bronson from WZID listened and heard that something that I had been wishing for someone to notice. I flew out, spending a weekend at the Wayfarer while they interviewed me and I did a short audition.

That first night in the hotel, I opened the window to look out over the pond and wondered what room Hunter S. Thompson stayed in when he covered the 1972 Presidential election for Rolling Stone magazine. I remembered him quipping about Manchester, the Wayfarer, and the primaries in New Hampshire in his book "Fear and Loathing on the Campaign Trail '72", it has become one of my favorite books because so much of it covers New Hampshire with the brutal honesty of a sharp outsider who understood what was really happening. I've remembered that book, and reread my copy several times since I started writing myself, hoping to quietly match that wit and judgment.

It wasn't until I eventually took over as the morning host on 96.5 the Mill that I finally decided I wanted to take writing seriously. I contacted Jeff Rapsis at the Manchester Express about writing a column.

We went to lunch and talked about my ideas, while Jeff patiently listened. I'm not sure what I said, but apparently, it was the right thing because he agreed to publish my column. I was ecstatic.

From that day, I saw the city with a new eye and dove into my writing. I started to see and look for things that I never noticed before. I bugged my friends and coworkers to read my columns, before and after they were published. They were excited, but probably more than a little annoyed. I'm sure my mother could relate.

I discovered a new side of myself. When something affected me, and I knew it was important or interesting, I wrote about it. When someone had a great story to tell, I wrote about it. When I saw something that was either noticed or unnoticed by the common eye, I wrote about it from my point of view. What I found is that my position or view isn't unique, but my voice is.

Writing this column is communicating to you the details of the the day... my day. When that is operating in its highest form, my column is a reflection of the city as well as a personal diary of my own view.

When it became clear to me that things were changing at the Express (and the venerable John Clayton temporarily left the Union Leader...) I found a new home at the New Hampshire Union Leader. It has been home ever since. I'm lucky to have this outlet and to use it each week to tell you what is going on and what I see.

In the time that I've had my "McCune's Manchester" column, I've watched as the turn of events effected myself and the city as a whole. Losing my job and learning the ropes of unemployment for nine months taught me valuable lessons. I've included a selection of those columns that dealt directly with those months and my experiences during unemployment. I've also included some of what I feel are the funnier columns to balance those hard times out. There's a selection of columns on people in the city, a selection of columns on places, and also a section about my family.

There are so many people who have helped in this journey. A big thank you needs to go out to them, including: John Toole, Ed Domaigne, Joe McQuaid, Jeff Rapsis, Mike Morin, Bob Bronson, Alex James, Deb Daigle, Kevin Cotter, Patti Ford, my friends, my wife, my children, my parents and the rest of my family who have made this happen... and mostly to you, dear reader. You are the one that this is all for.

Thank you. I hope you enjoy this book.

Funny

Looking for Manners? Avoid those Big-Box Stores

Oh boy, did I hit a nerve with this column. Somewhere between my pre-adolescent years and adulthood, we lost our manners. I suppose every generation thinks this. We mourn the loss of our "old ways" and suspiciously eye the "new ways" of the next generation. We are cautious, concerned and a little frightened that the world is passing us by and those things that were so precious in our youth will just seem stale and pointless as we get older.

I hope manners aren't one of those things. If you knew me in high school, you would probably be laughing at that statement now. But as I've aged and matured, I've come to a point where I appreciate manners more and more. I blame driving a car for that change in my life.

You've probably seen a collection of manner-less people every day you drive to work. Well, those people are going somewhere, and a lot of them shop at the big box stores. I don't blame the store, but the lure of low prices doesn't necessarily draw the best crowd. It draws everyone, and it takes all kinds.

What is silly is that I'm surprised when these type of things happen. The big, dumb guy and his kids getting in my way in this column, are unfortunately typical. For every dumb guy getting in my way, there is another yelling at a cashier at the grocery store, and yet another pretending they don't see you coming and "forget" to hold the door.

R.I.P., Good Manners. We mourn your loss more every day.

Comments from readers:

"I am a cashier at one of the big-box stores and am so sick and tired of people acting like I am not even there! I can't even walk down an aisle, without someone trying to walk thorough me, like I'm invisible. Unless of course, they need something.

When they come up to the register, they are either on their cell phones, (in which case, I do not make eye contact or speak), their kids screaming and pushing things at me so I can give it RIGHT BACK, and, of course, no such words like 'please' or 'thank you' is ever uttered from their little mouths.

And then, they actually THROW their items on the belt and heap everything so high, things fall off, and it's my fault that they fall on the floor.

Animals have better manners than some of us!

Boy, did you strike a nerve with me on your article, huh?

It's my day off and I just thought I'd write to you. Thank you for actually writing an article about how, we, as cashiers feel about manners.

Have a wonderful day and maybe some day manners will return! As they say, hope springs eternal.

- Sandi

We need more articles such as this, I can only hope the offenders can and will read them.
Thanks Adam.

- Paula

The box stores go out of their way to provide ultimate customer service due to the competition however they should try to impar(t) some manners to their customers. I was brought up by parents who taught me to open doors for women, (say) please and thank you etc. We did the same with our children and I am proud of their behavior anywhere. Your columns are a breath of fresh air.

- Paul

McCune's Manchester
August 6th, 2009

Sometimes, I give up hope for humanity as a whole.

Usually, I'm shopping at a big-box store when it happens. Without fail, when I'm in a Wal-Mart, Target, Lowe's, Home Depot, any grocery store chain in the area, and restaurants that are crowded, I end up getting angry with someone.

Some careless shopper will disregard every other person in the store and cut me off. Or perhaps another shopper will pretend to not hear me say "excuse me" when I try to get by them.

Or maybe one of their children will be screaming so loud that we have a hard time enjoying our meal and the parents act as if nothing is happening. It makes my blood boil. I want to stand up and chuck a salad fork at their table and yell, "knock it off!"

Argh! Stop it! I don't like feeling like this, but what has happened to all the decent people? Do we have any manners left?

I've found that there are very few of us manners-people left. We are a dying breed and we need to stick together. Rudeness rules the day. Rude people get to go first, they see what they want when they want to, and they don't feel any different for it. Maybe it's just me that is weird. Perhaps I'm the one who should change.

Next time I'm out shopping for falling prices, maybe I should just show up in my ketchup-stained sweat-pants, walk around, breathing through my mouth and getting in people's way, just to see how it feels.

I simply can't do it. I wouldn't be able to stand myself.

I tried in vain to get around this burly, sweaty man and his kids in a narrow aisle at the Bedford Wal-Mart. The store has been under a massive makeover lately, and the chaos is highlighting the behavior of the rude shoppers.

"Excuse me," I said. I was certainly loud enough for him to hear. One of his kids turned to look at me and stared. My first instinct was to just push through, ramming the cart into the burly-man's kidney. What would Emily Post do in this scenario?

After my third or fourth "excuse me," the man took a step forward. It was a step that had nothing to do with my polite tone or where I wanted to go. He just wanted to grab something from a higher shelf. So when I took this narrow window of opportunity, I sped with my cart to opening on the other side of this man's sweaty back.

He grabbed something on the top shelf, and just as I was behind him, he stepped back and right into my cart.

"Ooooh," I said, sucking air in between my front teeth.

"Ouch," he yelled back, his voice sounded like Andre the Giant on a bender, and it frightened and confused me. He glared at me as I walked by. I chalked it up to karma, I did ram the cart into his kidneys, only he did the dirty work.

The one place I've found freedom from the mass rudeness in a large gathering of people was an unlikely spot; the DMV.

Tuesday was my birthday, and I decided to spend an hour and a half celebrating with them.

Say what you will about the DMV, there is no questioning the order and authority of the place. You walk in, and go into the snaking line until you get to the front. If you're lucky enough to have to renew your license, as I did, you get to the front only to get a number to stand in another line.

"Why thank you for choosing to spend your birthday with us," said the woman behind the counter at the first line. "Not many people do that."

No, I suppose they don't. But I'm not most people. I watched most people at the DMV. They are the strange ones.

Most of them didn't stray from the Natural Order of Things. They would come in, as I did, and get in line. A few times, someone would just walk up to the counter and demand an answer. The woman at the counter would give a forced smile, (I have no doubt they teach this smile in training), and politely tell the man to grab a form and head to the back of the line. She could have easily told him to force the form into a certain part of his body and said as much, but she smiled at the man until he moved.

There is perfection in this model. Not once did some burly-man, or his brood, get in my way. I didn't have to put up with the careless nature of anyone, I only had to clutch my number and wait.

Emily Post once wrote, "Manners are a sensitive awareness of the feelings of others. If you have that awareness, you have good manners, no matter what fork you use." I agree. Next time, I will use any fork I choose to throw at the noisy table across the room.

Listening in on Life at the Park

You've seen these kind of people. Do you really need to smoke where there are children playing? This isn't Mad Men, and it certainly isn't 1959 any more. Maybe some people need a coming of age. Seriously, I try to see the good in everyone, but people make that really hard to do.

McCune's Manchester
May 15th, 2008

Who smokes at the park?

There are a few people. I know, I've seen them. Packs of mad-raving kids burning off the energy of a Happy Meal and high fructose corn syrup are crammed into a playground with their dull-eyed parents and a couple of people decide that right in the middle of the park is a good place to light up a butt.

Apparently, Livingston Park is part of flavor country.

You see a lot of amusement at our city's North End playground Mecca. But why would these two people think it's a good time to smoke right then?

To top it off, the conversation they were having was even better. I admit I was eavesdropping.

"I know you lit her cigarette, how come you did that?" Said the woman, who was clutching the cigarette between her fingers with the skill and precision of a seasoned smoker of 15 years. She was probably 25 years old.

"It's not like that, baby." The man said. He looked about the same age, but was dressed like a strip mall version of a white hip-hop artist, complete with saggy pants, his shirt off (revealing a "classy" shoulder tattoo) and his hat cocked to the side. Perhaps they were good people. Outward appearances would say otherwise.

The lady next to them inched her empty stroller away, carefully backing up and keeping them in her sights the entire time.

The smoker-woman got louder. "But you didn't need to light it for her!"

Good Lord. Here we go, I thought. I'm going to end up on Channel 9 tonight trying to stammer together a coherent thought about why these two knifed each other in between the swings and the slide.

"Well you see, Ray, they were talking about cigarettes and, well, gosh, the lady she just pulled out a knife and.. Well, I was over here and man, I don't know. Say, what's Tiffany Eddy really like?"

That's not the kind of exposure I wanted, time to move. Luckily the rest of Livingston Park has a lot to offer. I coaxed my two boys into a walk around the pond. My oldest needed the most prodding.

"Remember the long wooden bridge at the end?" I

told him.

His eyes lit up. "I can play Star Wars there!" he said, forgetting how much fun he was having. We made our way around the trail that mimics the shore. All the while, my boys are grabbing sticks and rocks and pretending they are various implements of destruction. A twig from an oak tree is easily a sword or gun to any boy. In fact... Everything is a gun. Michael Moore obviously never had a four year old son.

By the time we've made our way to the other end of the trail, my son figures out the biggest shortcoming of Livingston Park.

"I've got to pee." He declares and clutches his pants while starting the tell-tale dance. I've never been to Livingston Park when the bathrooms are open. Not once. I'm starting to think they are a front for some sort of Canadian gang who makes their money by selling unsanctioned Mary-in-the-half-shells. Or perhaps they open it under some well kept double-secret banker's hours.

So I did what any parent has to at some time; Find a shady patch of bushes and hope that's the worst of it.

Soon, the boys were getting tired. Their corn-syrup was wearing off as was my patience. We packed up the car and headed out.

The two smokers were still simmering in their anger on the bench. As I pulled out the car, he must have found the right combination of words as she fell into his shoulder and they embraced. Perhaps they weren't so bad after all.

It's All about the Meatballs

This column could have meant BIG trouble for me.

I was far too innocent to realize what I had done when I wrote this. I merely wanted to write a factual, blow-by-blow account of crashing the political after parties.

What happened after the story came out was incredible. I made a lot of people very upset, people I never intended to disturb in the first place. Readers wrote, called, and e-mailed the Union Leader. They were shaken by my tone, and at least one reader canceled his subscription because of this one column.

For anyone offended by this column, I want to apologize...even though I feel like I shouldn't. If you don't like it, read it again. I meant no disrespect to the process, or to the characters involved, I only wrote what I did and what I saw.

Basically, I was telling the reader what election night really is; a big party. It is a scene that most don't ever see. Instead, we are just casual, outside observers of a process that many feel is far too distant.

Joe McQuaid, the publisher of the Union Leader, forwarded me one such complaint e-mail. The reader was righteously angry that the story was put on page one. McQuaid certainly wasn't pleased with the overall tone he saw towards John Sununu, but he got it and actually defended me and my column. I'm still touched by that notion, and carry that story around with me to remind myself of where I am at.

I also remember that not everyone agrees with everything you say. That is important. McCune's Manchester is about as apolitical as a column can be. But that doesn't mean I leave politics to the John Distasos of the world. New Hampshire is still squarely in the public eye when politics are concerned, and if I'm going to write about New Hampshire, then I have to write about politics occasionally.

As for the Sununu's and the Shaheen's, well, I can only tell it like it is and how I saw it.

McCune's Manchester
November 16th, 2008

John Sununu was a big winner Tuesday night.

Well, it wasn't his night in the political sense. But he was the winner as far as victory parties are concerned.

You may have watched the results trickle in on WMUR. You probably saw a bunch of reporters spread out throughout the city, tucked away in banquet halls and convention rooms.

There's nothing worse, in the broadcasting world, than being stuck at the "Victory" party when it's obviously turning out to be the opposite. I always feel sorry for those reporters. It's the same feeling you get when watching a reporter interview the losing manager in the locker room after the World Series. No champagne here. Just a bunch of guys cleaning out their locker.

It's with that notion that a few of my friends and I head out every election night. We dress the part. Suits and ties, dress shoes and an attitude that we belong. We're in search of the party. Not the political party. The party with the best food.

Shallow? Maybe. One of my friends claimed we were "belittling the political process." Nonsense. We just wanted to see which candidate had the foresight to serve more than just chicken fingers. These things are important in the first 100 days after taking office.

Sununu beat everyone that night. Hands down. At the Wayfarer, he had a full spread of food. Supporters and covering press were treated to meatballs, turkey wraps and cheese tortellini in pesto. His cheese and fruit trays dwarfed his opponent's. It nearly made me forget all the negative advertising in the weeks leading up to election night.

Stand with President Bush? I don't care who did, did you try the meatballs? Those things were delicious.

Everyone was marveling at the food at Team Sununu. A cameraman winked and gave us a half-cocked smile as he walked by with a plate of tortellini. He knew.

It was a bizarre scene. There were depressed looks all around the room. Except from the elder Sununu, he was busy hectically typing on his Mac laptop and sharing tidbits with those at his table. The picture of all of this struck me as odd.

Our next stop was Murphy's Taproom. The crowd inside was diverse. It seemed like a strange place for Jeb Bradley's party headquarters. A van with a very big "Ron Paul" sticker was parked outside the Libertarian hot spot. During the primaries, this was the spot where Al Gore's television network, Current TV held their party. Funny how things change.

This was a very different crowd.

Our entrance was ill timed. We walked in immediately after a wave of exit polls came through. It wasn't looking good for Ole' Jeb.

Moments later, Bradley himself made an appearance.

He was wearing a bomber jacket. Now that's a real Maverick, I thought. We casually chatted with him.

"Nice spread." A friend of mine said to him.

Bradley laughed and said "I better get some of that." And walked over to his own cheese platter. I think he could see the writing on the wall. He's always seemed like a decent guy. Those people are the casualties of political campaigns.

The food was decent, with the usual fare. Still, Sununu had his fellow Republican beat.

Next, it was on to the Radisson, and our first encounter with the Party of Change.

In the crowd, skirts and suits were replaced with jeans and t-shirts. They were feisty inside, frothing at the mouth at the results on the giant television in the corner.

These people were sharks, and there was blood in the water. They could taste it. Obama had already been called the winner in the state. Shaheen had been declared the winner on our walk between Murphy's and the Radisson, and this crowd was ready.

But, there was no food to speak of. By contrast, there were more people here than the other parties. All that was left were the remnants of the cheese and fruit platters. I was disappointed. If Shaheen is an agent of change, next time I want to see a wider selection of food.

Shaheen held the same room at the Radisson that Rudy Guiliani booked for his primary party. It was another odd twist. Just a few months ago, the same room was the scene of Guiliani's assertion that he never planned on winning here. That night, I got the sense that they were warming up the jets to leave before the polls even closed in the Granite State.

The atmosphere on Primary night was very different from the one Tuesday in that same room.

Gathered at the back of the room, were a collection of cameras and tables for the assorted press. They outnumbered the press at the other parties by a 2 to 1 margin. Obviously, they had some sense of what was happening.

Our evening was drawing to an end. A few of my cohorts went to the Puritan to take in the Governor's party. It was already over for me. I drove home, taking it all in, wondering what all of it meant in the grand scheme.

Oh, and thank you John Sununu for the meatballs. They were delicious.

Signs of the Times

When I started collecting unemployment, I thought about this particular column and how crass it sounded in retrospect. Still, there is a funny angle the piece takes, and even going through that awful time of being unemployed, I still laugh when I read this.

McCune's Manchester
September 18th, 2008

I have a hot job tip for you.

You can work outside, meet lots of people, and also associate yourself with the collapse of our economy.

Sound exciting?

Have you thought about entering the world of standing-on-a-corner-holding-a-going-out-of-business-sign?

I've seen it more and more, and unfortunately, it appears to be the biggest growth area in our local economy. Furniture stores, jewelers, and lately "Linens N' Things" in Bedford. Apparently, 'N' Things' just aren't selling. Besides, they have to make way for yet another CVS/Walgreens/Brooks pharmacy.

If you want to become a sign-holder-guy, be sure to practice a few things.

First, you'll want to have the "I just rolled out of bed" appearance.

Please, also if you have a tattoo, make sure it's visible and at least slightly scary. Wear sunglasses, and a strange hat. In fact if the hat can be from an out-of-market football team and have some gaudy print to it, even better. Think "Cleveland Browns with a cow print" and you're on the right track. If you don't own one of these hats, simply use a dirty bandanna.

And be sure to be smoking and blowing the smoke in a creepy forced manner when an attractive lady in a BMW rolls by.

Basically, make it look like this is the only thing you can do.

Don't get me wrong, I have a lot of respect for these people and their ilk. Perhaps they come from a long line of "standing-holding-sign" people.

"My Grandfather held a going out of business sign before Montgomery took over for Wards!" They might say when pressed. You'll feel sheepish just for asking.

It takes a special breed to put up with the humiliation

of holding signs for money. I see the Little Caesar's pizza place on the West Side regularly has someone out, wearing or holding a sign advertising their "$5 anytime" pizza deal. Really? $5 pizza sounds a little suspect.

Every year at tax time, the ultimate humiliation comes up. Those poor people wearing the Statue of Liberty costumes for Liberty Tax Service. I laughed one time when I saw a man in one of those costumes smoking a cigarette. Did he realize the irony of holding a fake torch in one hand and a cigarette in the other?

Do they hold a convention? I can see them gathering at the Radisson, during the off-peak of Carnival season, to discuss new technologies in sign holding.

"One time, I stuck the stick in the ground and just stood by it. Collected my check with a smile." One enterprising sign-holder-guy might say.

We are a little more than a month away from the Superbowl of sign-holding; elections.

Every single polling station will be swarmed with McCain and Obama signs, being held in various degrees of happiness by different people. There will also probably be a handful of Nader people. None of them will be happy.

Doing some quick counting, you could see about a dozen people on any given day in our city doing this as their trade. What does that say about us? Holding a "going out of business" sign could be looked at as a cottage industry. Perhaps they should unionize.

"Oh, that's a Grand Opening sign. I only hold Going out of Business signs. If you don't like it, take it up with the Union Boss."

Sign Holders are here to stay, perhaps we should

recognize them. Maybe I shouldn't be so quick to pose the stereotype. It's a sign of the times that no one wants to hold.

Do Kids Today even Look in the Mirror ?

This is still a problem. Lately, I've noticed that nearly every high school boy has the same Jonas Brothers or Justin Bieber haircut. I guess things were the same when I was in high school. I look back at those pictures of me, and I was nothing more than a wannabe Kurt Cobain. I mention him in this story, and I recall his music having such a big impact on me. I've listened to it now, and it doesn't have the same appeal or zing to it.

What happened to me? When did I get so damned old? I don't mean to sound like T.S. Elliot, but I feel like getting older is all I talk about some days.

One night, during dinner, I turned to my wife and said "this salad is amazing!" Where did that come from? At what age does a salad seem like a 'yummy' meal?

And when did I start using the word 'yummy'?

McCune's Manchester
July 31st, 2008

Kids today.

Maybe I'm finally getting older. Or maybe it's a trend. But the way kids dress these days seems very odd.

Even as I write that, I can't help but imagine some

poor girl in the 1920's taking grief for her "flapper" look.

Every generation goes through its growing pains. But to me, kids today are generally bigger, lazier and dress worse than ever.

My evidence is everywhere. Take the mall, for example. More than a few times in the past month, I've hauled my two small boys to the Mall of New Hampshire for a respite from the heat. Every time we were given a sampling of trendy teenagers roaming its halls. Their fashion is always on display, usually funneling into stores like "the Limited 2" where they push low-cut tops to pre-teen girls. You can watch the parents cringe as their wholesome young girls walk in, only to return in the image of Britney Spears.

I thinks it's a sign of coming of age when you see your first repeat style, that awful look from when you were a kid that gets "brought back" because some pre-teen magazine says so. Like the bell-bottoms comeback, the four-inch rolled pant cuffs are everywhere all of the sudden. I remember in second grade, curling the bottom of my pants in one big fold. I'm nearly appalled to see it again.

It's the trend for tight fitting clothes that bothers me, perhaps more than it should. Like I said earlier, I think kids are a bit heavier than say 15 years ago. So why on earth would you want to highlight that? I've seen some of these packs of roving teenagers, poured into shirts about three sizes too small. It looks awful.

There's a term I've heard tossed around to describe it; Muffin Top. I'm not sure if that term describes how their belly fat hangs over their "low-rise" jeans or their diet. Either way the result is the same.

Don't get me wrong, I'm no underwear model. At least I don't highlight my lack of exercise. My fashion is far from the latest, in fact it's more of a uniform. Tee-shirt, blue jeans, sneakers and when it's cooler weather - a hoodie. I don't really veer too far from that. If you ever catch me out and about and I'm in a suit, it's either because I'm speaking at some event or trying to sneak into a function during the primaries.

The footwear today is also awful. I remember the girls back when I was a kid wearing "jelly shoes." I think they've come back in the form of Crocs.

Crocs are everywhere and have transcended kids. I know people who go to work in their bright yellow injection-molded footwear. Somewhere in India or China, there is a factory pooping these things out at the rate of 19,000 a second. Does that sound like sensible footwear to you?

At least the Crocs are sensible compared to those Heelie's that apparently went out of style last year. Those were the shoes with wheels in the heel. It was basically half a roller skate. There was nothing more annoying or frustrating that trying to sandwich into the aisles at Hannaford while some kid trailed his mother rolling by on those things. More than a couple of times, I had the urge to stick out my arm and clothesline a nine year old. How terrible is that?

I turn 30 next week. It seems like just yesterday I was trying on my first pair of baggy pants, and sliding into a Kurt Cobain styled flannel shirt. Both of those seem silly now, and that was 15 years ago. Today, the girls want to be Avril Lavigne, the boys want to look like a guitar player in an Emo band. There really isn't much distance between those two looks.

Just wait. Wait ten years when these same kids are rolling their eyes at the return of Heelies or the reincarnation of the Croc. I'll still be wearing my hoodie, taking my teenage boys to the mall and talking them out of whatever other awful styles have returned.

Parking Ticket Inspired him to take on City Hall

You win some, you lose some. A reader named "Rodney" from Cape Cod e-mailed me after this column came out. He was very angry:

> *What I certainly don't need to read is a long diatribe about how you got a parking ticket and why it is unfair because the pavement markings were covered. Moreover, instead of sounding like a spoiled brat with this sense of entitlement - exercise your due process methodically, and maybe justice will be served - as it was! You don't need to get up on a soapbox and bellyache in a disrespectful and sarcastic tone about how they can chase you with the yellow boot, etc. And why would you feel compelled to waste the time of a public servant in reading all that irrelevant nonsense? Do you think Parking Managers have nothing better to do than to sit there and read all that crap? I think the best resolution to all your chest pumping would have been to classify you as a "default" and suspend your driver's license and not bother chasing you anywhere. And when you get stopped by a police officer for a headlight out*

or something minor - you get carted away in the paddy-wagon for driving with a suspended license. Of course, in your world that would have been someone else's fault and readers would have had to endure another column of whining from you.

My response:

Sorry you took offense.
The parking manager found the humor in it, as was intended. I'm sorry you did not.
You literally wrote a lengthy e-mail about how I was being too whiny. I'm not trying to be snotty by pointing that out, but think about that for a second.
It was meant to be funny. I've had nothing but overwhelming support for what I wrote. Not that the masses are always right, but they tend to get it right most of the time.
Justice was served, I got out of my ticket and rightfully so. I believe that to be a direct result of the manner in which I wrote the city. I'm sure many other people have raised the same issue, the difference in my case was that something was done about it...and in my case, I changed a city policy on parking. In the grand scheme of things, that's tiny. In my world, that's huge.
In short: that letter did something.
Life is too short to be angry and do nothing about it. I decided to direct my anger into a form of humor and it worked. If we can't laugh, what do we have left?
I thank you for reading, even if you didn't appreciate it. I also thank you for taking the time to send me an e-mail. I know how much it takes to do that, and any and all

comments, good or bad, are always welcome.

- Adam

A short time later, he wrote back:

Your e-mail speaks volumes. We must admit our mistakes and I must admit that I may have misjudged you   and for that I am sorry. You are correct, life is too short and we must all preserve our sense of humor. I assure you   that I have always maintained one, although you probably   thought humor was the last quality that I possessed. If the   Parking Manager felt it was funny and took it in good   spirits - I may have misinterpreted or misread the intent.   In terms of the length of my e-mail, I of course was writing   to you and not to a public servant whose time should not   be wasted. (Not that I want to waste yours but public   input is something I presume you are accustomed to) We   completely agree on one thing. Taking the time to write   should be appreciated. The fact you did so regardless of   one's opinion says a lot about your open mindedness. So thanks for the response. I'm glad that the city was not   offended at your letter and I guess that I shouldn't have been either. I look forward to reading your articles in the future. You do have good writing skills!

I have to be honest, I don't mind getting these type of e-mails. Rodney was right, I was being kind of a jerk, even if there was a point to it.

The fact of the matter is that I helped change a city policy, if only for a season. The snow and ice from the winter of 2008-2009 was immense. Our driveway had two end caps that I measured at 11 feet at one point. It seemed that we would just pick up after one snow storm only to prepare for the next. By January, when this happened, I was ready to give up.

When this incident occurred, I just happened to be with an attorney. I almost included that in the story and my letter, but didn't. Honestly, I thought it would make me sound guilty of something, which wasn't true.

Still, Brandy Stanley, the Parking Manager for the city does an excellent job. She has one of those hard positions to hold. Who likes meter maids? (and they hate that term..) This letter, and this column opened the door to a great working relationship with this city department.

So read the column, take it with a grain of salt and chuckle, like I did.

McCune's Manchester
January 22nd, 2009

They say you can't fight City Hall. While that may be true in some sense, the following is a letter I sent to the city concerning a recent parking ticket, and their official response. Portions of both letters have been edited for length. My effort was successful:

I was greeted on Friday by one of your lovely orange envelopes on my car door. I can't thank you enough.

I thought I had done everything right on that day. I got out, dutifully parked immediately in front of a shiny new parking kiosk on Central Street. Put in my card, punched up the maximum time and even came back to my car a full ten minutes before my time had come up.

Good Mr. Citizen.

So why did I have one of those lovely orange presents under my wiper? I was within 15 feet of a fire hydrant.

I have no doubt that this is a grandfathered city ordinance, if not an outright tradition. For sure it's an easy money maker, because I didn't have the tape measure and video camera that's needed to document such an incident. I understand, times are tough and every effort needs to be made to raise some much needed capitol. But why me?

I called and heard you took a picture of my car. Lovely isn't it? Which do you like best? Its classic German Diesel engineering? Its boxy European headlights or the stylish tones coming from its muffler when it starts up. I'm partial to the later, though you probably weren't there to appreciate that aspect of my classic 300TD. Which, by the way, you labeled a "MERZ STWG" on your ominous parking violation. Is this a new form of texting?

Anyway, to the point. I can't really dispute how far away I was from said fire hydrant. I can say that, short of knowing the exact detail of the ordinance, there would be no way to know what to expect. That and our recent downfalls of snow have slightly obscured the hydrant in question.

Surely, had the road been cleared underneath that ugly rotten ice and snow, it would have revealed a cross-hatch pattern, indicating "no parking." I'm not blaming the plow guys, those poor people have worked enough, I'm just saying I would have parked elsewhere. In fact, there were other spaces. I simply chose the one closest to the kiosk. Who would expect that's not a "legal" space?

Does that picture you took include the lack of a proper sign? Does it show the crusted snow on top of the road, making it impossible to see any tell-tale road markings?.

At any rate, some sort of sign-age is necessary here. I don't think anything short of that is sufficient.

Until that sign is in, I just don't feel comfortable paying this ticket. I'd rather donate $50 to the Food Bank. Lord knows they could use it.

I'd also be happy to send a check for the full amount owed ($50) immediately with one condition: that it is earmarked specifically for a sign saying something like "Read All Ordinances" or "Danger: Meter Maid Loitering Area." Or even simply, "No Parking." I'm assuming that last one is probably better. It seems more suited for public service.

Otherwise, I won't pay. I'm telling this to you with certainty. You can hunt me down, like a dog, wasting countless hours on wages and gasoline in vehicles and watch your blood pressure rise as you spend thousands of dollars lugging around a yellow boot all in the name of my $50, or we can come to some sort of mutually beneficial agreement.

So, in case my intention has been obscured in this lengthy diatribe, let me state this clearly: I'm formally asking for a review of my ticket.

Thanks,
Adam McCune

Dear Mr. McCune,

I received your parking ticket dispute for the above citation, and I recalled speaking with you on the phone some time back. First, let me say that we have already voided your parking ticket, as the pictures taken at the time the ticket was issued do indeed show that the striping is covered in ice and the vehicle was parked directly in front of a Pay & Display meter.

During wintertime, we do receive some disputes of this nature, and we always try to fairly resolve each situation. The PCO's out in the field generally take snow and ice into consideration when deciding to issue a ticket. In some cases there is a difference of opinion and when we receive disputes, management and enforcement staff discuss them as a group to determine a fair and consistent method of enforcement.

With regards to your suggestion about sign-age, we do our best to reduce the amount of visual noise (or "stuff") on the sidewalks, and a large percentage of that "stuff" is sign posts. We have found that when there is snow and ice obscuring the striping in that area, people don't park illegally. Most winters, the street is clear up to the curb and we haven't had a problem. So, rather than install more sign posts, we will opt to take it easy on enforcement this winter and see what happens next winter.

Brandy Stanley
Parking Manager
City of Manchester

Dad finds Drama at the Bus Stop

Oh, the bus stop. The day this column came out was the last day my son and I went to the bus stop.

Not because the parents or the kids read the column, but because I realized nothing had changed and nothing ever would.

A part of me hoped the parents would read this particular column, see the error of their ways and perhaps change their behavior. Not a chance. Those same parents were absent again that particular morning, and their kids were as unruly as ever. What a fool I was to think I could impart change.

The sad fact is that irresponsible people are ignorant. One reader, who's email is below, pointed out to me that the people I was talking about probably don't read the paper. They're right.

> *Recently, I was talking to my neighbor with my 1 yr old and their kids. In the meantime, a car came speeding (it wasn't really that fast) but one of the Mom's went and stopped the car and yelled at them!!! I was amazed and impressed! That's exactly what needs to be done in these circumstances.*
>
> *Maybe you could try and talk to some of your neighbors about it - so that the parents are more aware of the situation, and the sometimes unacceptable behavior that happens there.*
>
> *Keep up the good work! I'm proud to have people like you in our community!*
>
> *— Mike*

I have to tell you.....I LOVED your article today. I say it often, where in the world are the parents????? Drives me nuts. I, too, have stepped in, disciplined, etc., but I have four kids of my own and I feel like, I'm supposed to raise your kid too?? We must be close to the same age because just the other day I said I NEVER would have talked to an adult the way kids do today. I had respect....okay....fear, really, but what has happened to that? Sad part is the parents who are dropping their kids off, probably aren't reading the newspaper.......maybe we can hand out your article at the bus stops :)
Have a great day! Thanks for validating my feelings.

- Kim

I have a 2 yr daughter. She is two going on 16. So, I can not fully relate to the bus stop but I have seen similar situations at parks, children sporting events, and stores. The children run loose around and the parents don't even know where the kid is. Next thing you know, the child comes back hurt or crying and the parent is like what happened? Well, you would know if you were watching or god forbid Parenting. I have in a few instances told children to behave or if they wanted to do that please go somewhere else.

Thanks for the article,

- Tim

McCune's Manchester

October 29th, 2009

The school bus stop is as close to complete chaos as I care to get.

I walk down with my first grader before school, and at times, I'm the only adult there.

Sometimes, there is one more adult; he usually sits and stews in his big truck, watching the theater unfold from his windshield.

And make no doubt, it is theater. There is tragedy, romance, heartache, and joy unraveling every morning between 7:30 and 7:38. For me, though, it's torture.

In today's world, I don't know my place. What am I to do when kids are acting up around me and I'm the only adult? Is it up to me to punish them and keep the order?

Last week at the bus stop, two kids stole another kid's hat. They ran around, tossing it back and forth, playing keep away to the distressed kid. I stepped in. Told them to stop it, and they gave the hat back. When the "victim" got his hat back, he threw it in the face of one of the perpetrators, a little girl who seemed to enjoy being chased.

"Hey, don't do that," I said. "You wanted the hat back, and you got it."

"Shut up, I hate you," the first grader said back to me. I glanced up and the man in the truck was shaking his head. Was he shaking his head at me, or the kid's behavior? Rest assured, I would never have gotten away with such a statement when I was a first grader.

My mind has wandered while these kids act up. I can picture some parent coming down in a huff one morning, to confront me for "talking that way" to their innocent little child, throwing out things like "how dare you," and "I would never" without batting an eye at the irony of such statements.

The bus finally came, and I left for work, passing another bus stop where some older kids were waiting. I've passed this same spot before, watching junior high aged kids smoke a cigarette before they get on the bus.

The lack of parenting doesn't begin or end at the bus stop. Seeking an alternative, I dropped my son off at school one morning. A mother of a girl in my son's class waits outside for the school to open every morning. She said that if she stands and waits outside, instead of in her car, parents leave their kids with her. They just walk away, presumably going to work.

A woman who lives near Memorial High School (and wishes to remain anonymous) has seen far worse.

She snaps pictures of kids, standing on the street outside her window, smoking from a glass pipe before heading out to school. Like they need a hit of crack before heading out to math class. She sends these pictures to the principal, hoping for some action.

She came home one day to find two teenagers, as she says "going to town" on her front lawn after school. She said she thought about following the girl home to tell her parents, but worried about getting in trouble for stalking, which is unfortunately true.

We live in a world that is served by several masters. Most of them operate simultaneously, usually in exact conflict of one another. People are litigious, especially if that perceived slight is aimed at their children. Yet these same people don't seem to see the merit in accompanying their children to the bus stop.

What is the role of someone like me, or someone like the mother waiting for the school to open, or the woman who catches kids doing nefarious things on and/or around her lawn? Are we responsible for other people's children? Or next time, should I just let them keep the hat?

Open Mic Comedy: Entertainment and a Dream

I have a love-hate relationship with comedy, particularly stand-up comedy. The love is the laughter. I enjoy that. I always have.

The hate is some of the people involved. The people who do comedy are ego driven. They are self-centered, arrogant jerks.

I am not unlike them, and when two people of that nature collide, the result is usually not pretty.

In this column, I basically try to give the reader an overview of what the comedy night at the Shaskeen, or any open-mic venue, is like.

McCune's Manchester
April 10th, 2009

"They're all going to laugh at you."
That's the title of Manchester native Adam Sandler's debut comedy CD from 1993. For some, the idea of someone laughing at them isn't a bad thing.

Somewhere behind Sandler, Sara Silverman, and the Meyers brothers, rest the hopes of a new generation of Manchester comics.

These people have day jobs. Some might be accountants, others students. One might just be the guy who bagged your groceries or put on your summer tires.

Wednesday nights at the Shaskeen on Elm Street, Nick David and Brad Hagen host a smattering of comics on all levels. The open-mic there has been going on for several months, seeing dozens of comics of various levels. For the audience and the performers, the open-mic has followed the unwritten rules laid down by Boston area comedians over the years.

#1 - Don't charge a cover at open mics.

Comics hate this. The reason? It's not a "comedy" show in the sense of going to see Bob Marley or Jimmy Dunn at the Palace. Those shows are polished presentations, the result of years of touring, writing, and rewriting every word of their tried and true jokes. Open-mic comedy is not that. If someone walks in, pays a cover charge and sees a terrible comedian, as a consumer they tend to lump in the failure of a newbie as a condemnation of the comedic art as a whole. Sometimes you'll get a pro comic working out material, but the other 99% of the time, it's someone who's trying to figure out how the game works.

#2 - Anyone can go up.

I've been to several "shows" at the Shaskeen, and in that time, I've seen at least six comics get on stage for the first time. It's wonderful and awful at the same time.

The courage it takes to get in front of people and bare your soul is amazing, but it's also obvious some people have it and some people don't. To me, the uncomfortable feeling of watching someone nervously wait for a laugh that's not ever coming is one of the strange pleasures of open-mic comedy.

#3 - Reward.

At the end of the night, Nick and Brad give a $50 reward to the night's funniest comic. It's an unscientific decision between the two hosts who make the decision based on "who makes them laugh the most."

On any given night, 15 comics go on stage and spew their five minutes of funny. It can be crude humor and often it is. Comedians such as Billie Joe occasionally do dirty joke laden parody songs with the help of a guitar, others, like Matt Farley stand up to sit down at their keyboard and play their quirky clean comedy songs on piano. For most, like Kevin Cotter, it's just a matter of standing with the microphone between them and the audience.

There is nothing more thrilling to a comedian than the power of an audience laughing at you. No where else does this phenomena happen. Imagine all your coworkers, facing you, holding beers and mixed drinks and laughing. It isn't comfortable to think of for most. But for an aspiring comedian, it's a goal. It's that driving force that compels cashiers and cooks, bartenders and salesmen to get on that stage, grab the mic and share with the crowd their life's experience. It's beautiful really. A crowd of strangers share in the moment.

It's a comfortable setting for an open-mic, with the performers and audience mingling in the same room. It makes the comics seem close and approachable because they are.

I've been on stage at the open mic several times. A while back, I had tried my hand at comedy with a small level of success. I, like most of the others on that stage on any given Wednesday, am trying to reach that level of success. It's a long progression.

First you do the open-mic, then you get asked to perform at a "booked" gig, which is nothing more than an open-mic with a waiting list. After that, you open for a moderately well-known regional comedian. You network some more and work your way to being the second fiddle on a larger-named bill. Beyond is a whole world of headlining, Comedy Central specials and corporate gigs. Most of the comedians on stage last night won't get any closer to that than they would by buying a ticket to "real" show somewhere else. But that won't stop them, and it won't stop me.

I like it when people laugh at me.

People

His Dad's Gone, so Kevin's Hitting the Road

Kevin Cotter has been a friend of mine pretty much since the moment I arrived in Manchester. That was in 2004. When I first met him, I thought he was at least ten years older than me. He's actually five years younger.

Almost from the moment I knew him, he had a giant beard and scally cap. There were moments where he ditched the hat or the beard, but they always come back. Now, it's almost part of his overall persona.

Going through the experiences that we went through, individually and together, really did cement our friendship.

When Kevin's dad passed away, it came after the end of a long fight. It was tough on Kevin and his sister, but it was time.

His father had suffered too long.

In the end, Kevin has yet to go anywhere. In fact, I would say his father's death has almost tethered him to Manchester. Since this article came out, Kevin has been promoted at work, been honored with accolades for his stand-up comedy, and even moved in with his girlfriend.

It's almost the opposite of what he thought would happen.

Still, there is a wanderlust I see in his eyes. It's a familiar gaze, and certainly not foreign to the American heart; that moment where eyes drift to a distant horizon full of future stories and possibilities. Ears and nose go on alert, as if they are a dog preparing for the hunt.

Because they are. We hunt down the road and its endless possibilities because we must. It is human to run to a new destination, brimming with hope and aching with loss.

Someday, I hope Kevin finds that peace, whether it's here or in the distance.

McCune's Manchester
August 13th, 2009

Everybody has a catalyst that changes their lives. For Kevin Cotter, that catalyst is the death of his father.

Kevin has been a friend of mine since I moved to the city five years ago. In that time, we've been through a mountain of events. Some good, some bad, and their collective magnitude has cemented our friendship.

When you go through similar moments as a friend of yours, it has a way of drawing you closer. In the past five years, I went through a divorce while Kevin's fiancé broke off an engagement. When Kevin started an open-mic comedy night, I was right their with him, and watched as the venue turned greedy, ending its tenure there.

I've mentioned Kevin a few times in this column, usually as a "teetotaler." He gives me grief for hanging the title on him, as if there is any shame in it.

Well, I can tell you that statement isn't totally true. Kevin got miserably drunk the night he learned his father, Ricky Cotter, had cancer. That was a couple of years ago now, and last week, Kevin's dad passed away. It's one situation I don't know how to relate to, both of my parents are still alive and well.

His father was an ornery guy, and I mean that in a good way. Those are the type that always have the biggest fight in them, and there were several times that it looked like he was kicking cancer. On five separate occasions, the doctors were astounded to find that no cancer was showing up in their fancy tests. They scratched their heads, looking at charts in disbelief.

Still, the doctors handed him a death sentence several times.

"Mr. Cotter, you've got two months to live," they would say. Six months later they would say it again. A year later, they would give their two month sentence another shot. Last week, after three years of guessing, they finally were right.

I don't know which is a harder way to lose someone close. If it happens suddenly, you're haunted by your last moments together. The last words exchanged have a habit of hanging around in the air, bouncing around in your head. But the long-kiss-goodnight could be the worst. You have to watch them suffer. What was once your strapping father is now a frail reminder in a hospital bed.

Maybe that's why Kevin wants to take off. He's talked about packing his stuff in a storage locker and set out to work for his company in Chicago, with a wanderlust fueled by a question he can't answer: why?

I don't know the answer, and I don't know if Kevin will find the answers in Chicago, Illinois, or Big Sur, California, or Topeka, Kansas. All I can say is that I don't blame him. Sometimes, we have to stick around and endure the pain, other times, we need to run. It's not cowardice, it's actually the opposite. Kevin is taking a break from the harsh times he's lived in the last few years. There is a certainly a romantic notion to the idea. We've had a fascination with the road in America, and being on the East coast means the rest of the country is spread out like a map, full of possibilities to the west.

So, as Kevin seeks his Manifest Destiny, I hope he finds what he's seeking and that he can leave some of the sorrow behind.

Kevin had the courage to give a eulogy at his father's funeral on Monday. "If you knew my dad," Kevin said, "you knew he liked westerns. I asked my dad who the toughest man was and he told me, 'John Wayne.' Well, John Wayne beat cancer twice, my dad beat it five times, so my dad was tougher than John Wayne."

Turning Tragedy into a Neighborhood Revival

I love Cheryl Mitchell's story. She is a staple in her community, and I think we all benefit from people like her, but rarely recognize their efforts.

She's inspiring, righteous, caring, clever, cautious, and daring all in one.

For those of us (myself included) who always say, "I don't have the time!" Cheryl Mitchell is a reminder that we do.

McCune's Manchester
July 17th, 2009

Cheryl Mitchell has always had a big heart.

Mitchell is a life-long Manchester resident and her big heart is evident in her dogs. One was a stray pit-bull she took into her home, the other two are tiny chihuahuas, one of them rescued from a hoarding situation. In October of 2006, you could say those things defined the 54 year old's giving nature. That was before Officer Michael Briggs was shot in the yard of her Lake Avenue home.

The day after the shooting, she stood in her yard with about 30 other people, all staring at the fresh-cut flowers left by strangers. She talked to the people, and asked how many were from Lake Avenue. She was shocked when most of the people raised their hands and she didn't recognize any of them.

It was then she decided to stop being a stranger and start being a neighbor.

"When I was a kid, I would walk by and say 'good morning' or 'good evening'," she told me, having lived in that same neighborhood for most of her life. "We don't do that anymore and I thought 'why don't we?'" So, after the shooting, she started the simple chore of greeting people. Most would give her strange looks, but some started saying 'hello' back. Shortly after, she started a neighborhood watch.

Her group would stroll the streets, keep an eye on the neighborhood and talk to its people. Soon, it became much more than just a neighborhood watch, as they heard the concerns and issues of the residents. Now, it's called Eagles Eyes Community Organization.

Soon, she started an effort to clean up the local skate park, and after listening to a group of people on Blodgett Street who were sick of the graffiti, she put a plan in action. It started with garage doors.

"What would happen if we maybe put murals on garages?" she said. "That way people would be able to go down an alley and look at a really beautiful mural and not graffiti." It was a novel approach; murals as anti-graffiti. Last year, Mitchell says they painted 17 garage doors. She has an army of volunteers, but says some people are having a hard time committing, even though they offer the murals for free.

They are in the planning stages of a very large mural, one that would equal the size of the beautiful mural painted on the side of the Quizno's building near the YMCA downtown. She is as dedicated as she is ambitious.

Did she ever picture doing this? "Absolutely not," she told me. At least not until that awful morning in October of 2006, when an officer, a man she only knew in passing, was gunned down on her lawn. It's still hard for Cheryl to say that she's doing something so good only because of something so terrible. A man's life, a father, a husband, was ended so close to her home. Yet, it became a catalyst that's taken over her life. It seems she has a hard time feeling good about her efforts, telling me that it "hurts her heart." There's almost a guilt she hangs on her ambition, perhaps it drives her further.

"I call it God's will," she said, "some people don't like religion, so I just say it's fate." Whatever you call it, she's done something. The fact that any good can come out of that event is amazing. Through this tragedy, there is hope.

Mitchell's ultimate goal is to open a community center. Her vision is a place where people can come in an open door and enjoy their time. A place where the young and old can meet and gather and enjoy the space equally. It's a vision that represents all of her memories of a wonderful neighborhood from her childhood. These visions of riding bike until dark, with neighbors who knew your name and people who watched out for each other seems so simple, but still so far off. She fears it won't happen, even admitting that she doesn't think it ever will. I think, with her ambition, anything is possible.

This week, Mitchell's big pit bull passed away after suffering from leg problems, an unfortunately common ailment for dogs of that breed. For a woman with such a big heart, it saddens me to think she lost something she considered to be so close. Maybe that's the danger in being a person who cares.

Roger Lacerte, a Winner in any Language

This column has such a back story, it's worth writing this entire book just to tell it.

When this column came out, I received a call on my cell phone. Not recognizing the number, I decided to screen it and let it go to voice mail.

I was appalled at the message that was left.

"This message is for whoever wrote that article about that awful Roger LaCerte," a woman's voice screamed out. She sounded old, frail, and extremely pissed off.

"I don't think you should write about such people, especially as someone who is French. He is not, he's Acadian!" What in the world is 'Acadian'? I thought.

I looked it up. More or less, Acadians were persecuted people, exiled by the French speaking population in early Canada and Maine. It's a proud heritage, with roots deep into Maine and New Hampshire (Acadia National Park near Bar Harbor, Maine, for instance.) With my quick history lesson in tow, I felt I had the proper ammunition to argue my case.

I called the lady back.

"Who is this, and how did you get my number?", the voice said back on the other end. I recognized it as the woman from my voice mail.

"I guess I could say the same thing, this is Adam McCune, and you called me and left a rather disturbing message on my phone," I said, already getting my vinegar up. She started in immediately.

"Oh," she paused. "Oh, YOU," she said in a scathingly angry tone, closer to the Wicked Witch than the Good One.

"Roger LaCerte is not French, he's Acadian," she said triumphantly.

"What's the difference?"

"What's the difference? Acadians are awful people, do you know their past?"

"No," I lied. I was more than curious now, I was hooked.

"Acadians are awful, terrible people and don't deserve to be called 'French'" she said. I was wondering if this was some terrible joke, set up by one of my friends.

"They'd steal the shirt off your back if they could!" Jesus, I thought, who is this person, and where does her bigotry end?

"Well, even if you are right-"

"-I am right!"

"Even if you are right, Roger has served the French community well and deserves the recognition he's getting. Besides, if you are going to hold his heritage against him, you are going to call me a barbarian and a savage, because I'm part Scottish and part Cherokee Indian," which is true. I was only egging her on.

"You're what?" she asked, sounding like she was reaching for a piece of paper. Suddenly, I felt the urge to hang up.

"Plus Roger never plays any requests on his show," she stated. Now it started to become clear, she was an angry listener who felt spurned. I knew this game well, and I had all the cards, while she probably wasn't playing with a full deck. Time to bring this show to an end, I thought.

"Say, where did you get this number?" I asked.

"I looked it up in the phone book."

"Lady, this is a cell-phone," I said. I heard a click at the other end.

McCune's Manchester
April 23rd, 2009

A vinyl record hisses as it meets the needle on the turntable. The sound is matched with the hiss of an old AM transmitter, throwing out the hisses laced with musical notes and words in French.

"Bon Jour," a voice says warmly.

A driver in a car tuning the radio while traveling on 293 might mistake the sound as a wayward signal lost in the atmosphere between Montreal and Manchester. In fact, it's derived right in Manchester, a stones throw from the Merrimack River.

Roger LaCerte has hosted the French-language program "Chez Nous" on AM 1370, WFEA since 1998.

Roger followed in the traditions laid out by Joe Maltais and later Paul Pare at the radio station. It's a labor of love for him.

For years, I would see Roger occasionally roaming the halls at my old radio haunt. To me, he was simply known as "that French guy." I'll admit, I have listened to his show only occasionally. I never took French, so his words are literally foreign to me. I know, that admission could be considered blaspheme were I to move to certain neighborhoods on our city's West Side.

The most interaction I've had with Roger over the years is usually bumping into him on a Sunday morning while he hauls his boxes of CD's and old records up the elevator and down the hall, parking himself squarely in front of the microphone, spilling his lovely French limericks over the air. Occasionally, I've passed him along the way to the bathroom or snack machine. Always, he says "hello" in one language or another.

French-language programming isn't exactly the most lucrative entity a person can venture into. But for him, I think the show and his involvement in it is worth more than dollars or Francs or Euros.

Roger runs a book store on Orange Street called La Libraire Populaire. As you could probably guess, it's a French-language book store. He also sells greeting cards. He's taught French on every level, from elementary students to college nearly every year since 1957. The language is so ingrained in him, he greats everyone as though he were in the Old City section of Montreal.

"Bonjour," he would say as we passed in the hall. His smile is contagious and warm. There's a happiness to it that few people have, a charm that is both spirited and positive.

Next month, the Manchester Historical Society is honoring Roger for his commitment the French heritage of our city. Roger will be given the Conservation of Cultural Resources award during their Historic Preservation ceremony. I can't think of anyone more deserving. Perhaps it should be called the Roger Lacerte award, considering his status is close to that of a missionary for the city's Franco-American community.

I remember how forward that heritage was when I first moved to the city. I set up a bank account at Saint Mary's Bank, the building itself being a monument to the area's French heritage. I don't know how many times I stood in line trying to pick my way through the words beneath the giant mural on the wall on the McGregor Street branch. It's all in French, with a picture to help those like me understand that it was about the native people and the settlers that chose the banks of the Merrimack river to be their new home. I wondered if those people in the mural ever envisioned a banking institution with wild technologies and machines that dispensed cash through computers. Computers that still ask users if they prefer "English" or "Francais."

It's that past that comes alive in Roger's voice every time he speaks into the microphone in that lonely studio. Except that he's not totally alone. Roger takes calls. Lonely widows and students, lifelong residents and passers-through that hear the show call in with their requests.

After Roger accepts the award, the next time I see him, I'll just have to say: "Bien fait."

How I Fought through Black Friday

I'm not much of a shopper, at least not for presents. When it comes to a big purchase for myself, I research and research until I find just the right item. This is especially true when it comes to electronics.

But when I'm shopping for toys, especially The Big Toy for Christmas, I have issues. My frugal nature forces me to check the Sunday paper's ads and try to translate names like "Dragonoid" and "Picachu" from nonsense into common, adult English.

This in itself is a feat of accomplishment.

I searched and searched for these coveted toys, and none were to be found. I understand business enough to know that one thing you want to create, if you are making something like a Bakugan, is scarcity. But how shameful is that? To create a toy that children love so much, yet make fewer of them just to make a buck and create a buzz.

In the end, what happened after this column was a true gift of the season.

McCune's Manchester
December 4th, 2008

What was I thinking?

I went shopping on Friday. Black Friday. The aim was to get a jump on the Holiday. And like you, I was attracted by the amazing prices. The lure of buying a toy for $9 as opposed to $25 was just too much. I soon realized the fallacy of my logic.

I pulled into a parking space at the Toys R Us near South Willow Street, not ready for what was ahead.

The place was packed. Shoulder to shoulder with other parents, all with the same look of desperate delusion that comes with shopping on that fateful day.

I made a rookie mistake. I grabbed a cart. My youngest son was with me and the treachery of trying to keep an eye on him and fight the other parents was too much.

And fight I did. Seriously. I never thought I would be in the middle of one of those stories you hear about, but there I was.

With apologies to Edward R. Murrow, it seemed I was reporting from the front lines.

A woman raced by me with three or four packages of Bakugans in her hand. To this day, I'm still not exactly sure what a "Bakugan" is, other than my son really wants them for Christmas. They appear to be small balls that transform into robots when thrown down. This is some part of an elaborate game. To me, they look like something that came out of a gum-ball machine. To my son, they are treasure.

I asked the woman where she found them.

"Hands off!" She shouted and gave the dirtiest look I've ever seen.

Apparently, she forgot this was the time of year when visions sugar plums should dance in her head.

I stood there frozen for a moment, trying to react to the woman's response. A friend of mine saw me across the aisle. She shouted something about having a strange look on my face. I was about ten feet away from her, but I knew that if I wanted to go over and talk to her, it would take about 20 minutes to get to her. Kind of like driving in Boston. You can see where you want to be but have no idea how to get there.

This was 15 or 20 minutes into my shopping experience and already my frustration was through the roof. Later, when I heard the story about the Wal-Mart employee in New York who was trampled to death, I was not surprised.

Nor was I shocked when I heard that people at that same Wal-Mart refused to leave when they decided to close the store after realizing what happened. Why should they leave? I mean, it's just a man dying. Happens everyday. But a $100 portable DVD player for only $50? That's once in a lifetime!

It's basic here, really. What we need is a little decorum. A little common sense, and without trying to sound too corny, a little Christmas spirit. I left the craziness of the store behind and headed to the mall where my results were not any better.

I spent 30 minutes driving in a loop around the parking lot. Desperation takes over and I decided to follow a woman coming out of the store with six bags in her hand.

I basically stalked her to her car and waited for her to unload her treasures and drive off.

But she carefully packed her loot away, closed the door and walked back into the mall. She could have easily waved me through. I know she saw me, how could she miss a guy in a 25 year old car that burns diesel and stinks about as much as you can imagine. Plus I still had that "look" stamped on my face. A simple wave and her pointing back to the mall would have sent me on my way. Instead, I was forced to sit and breath those lovely fumes out of my car. At least I wasn't trampled to death.

Grudgingly, I pulled away and found a distant spot on the other side of the mall. Skillfully pushing my son in a stroller I made my way inside. I bought one item and was done. Again, I was met with a pitiful lack of those coveted Bakugan.

Seriously, the people who make them are smart. They look like they are produced by some giant machine capable of pooping them out at a rate of a million a second. Instead, they turn the knob on that machine way down to slow, or perhaps stop. Then they sit back and laugh as parents scramble to buy up these silly things at a 1000% markup.

I was told by my coworker, Heather, a Black Friday veteran, that there were certain rules I broke. A Natural Law that pertains to Black Friday shopping.

The most serious of these offenses was my apparent bulk in cargo.

I had a child with me, it weighed me down. Pushing a stroller does not compute with Black Friday shopping. The idea is to travel light, like the natives. Blend into their environment.

Heather does not even carry her precious purse. She ditches it in favor of a wallet. I might consider a money clip next year for its aerodynamic properties.

Or maybe next year, I'll skip it all together. For people like Heather, Black Friday is the opening of hunting season, or opening day at Fenway.

As a nation, we spent about 7% more this Black Friday as opposed to last. If there was an economic turn-down, it wasn't apparent at the stores in Manchester on Friday.

Now if I could just find that Bakugan.

Reader's Gifts Speaks to the Magic of Christmas

This is what happened a week after my search for Bakugans came up empty handed. I still don't know who the mystery person was. The fact that they did this anonymously warms my heart.

McCune's Manchester
December 11th, 2008

It was about 8am last Friday when one of my coworkers came into the studio.

He had a package in his hand. It was a paper bag and it had my name scribbled in marker on the side.

"This must be for you." He said with a surprised look on his face.

Inside was something I never expected, and it reminded me what Christmas was all about. I'll come back to that in a moment.

First, let's back up. Last week in my column, I wrote about my troubles of shopping on Black Friday.

One woman in particular irked me. She was holding three packages of a most-coveted toy. Bakugan Battle Brawlers. They also happen to be something my five year old son desperately wants to have under the tree in a couple of weeks. When I asked her where she got them, she flashed an evil look my way and said "Hands off". The incident left a bad taste in my mouth.

They are impossible to find. After the column came out, I was pointed towards a few places online that still carried them in stock. Those kind readers helped me find the coveted toy. But it was what was inside this package that reminded me of when I was five and Christmas was still magic.

Inside, were two Bakugan and a note that said:

"Some of us are still good at Christmas. Hope this is what you looking for. Merry Christmas from a reader."

I sat in silence for a couple of seconds, staring at the note and the gift from my anonymous Santa. It made me realize how much I had forgotten.

I remembered what it was like on those Christmas Eves not so long ago. The anticipation was a killer. My brother and I would wake up, sometimes around three or four in the morning and sneak downstairs to see what was under the tree.

How did that sled get here? Where did this package come from? It was from Santa Claus. Then, sometime after Saturday morning cartoons lost their luster and girls started to smile at me, I stopped believing in Santa as a person and I lost that magic.

Well, I'm here to say "Yes Virginia, there is a Santa Claus." And he obviously knows where I work.

The gift itself was simple enough. It didn't cost a lot for someone to buy those two Bakugan. What it did cost was time. I'm blown away that someone would get in the car, drive to Wal-Mart, buy the gift, put it in a bag, write my name on it and drop it off at the door. The fact that they are not something that stays on the shelf makes me wonder if it was an inside job.

It's amazing how a token gift or gesture can go so far. And it can be simple. Let someone go in front of you on Elm Street. Next time you have a cart-load of groceries at Stop and Shop, and the guy behind you only has a bottle of wine, let him through. He obviously has some place to be. It's a basic recognition that someone else exists. That they can just "be". Sometimes that's the biggest gift of all.

As long as there is a gift, children don't lose that magic until just before those teen years. That's why I have to take those toys and drop them off at a Toys for Tots bin. My son doesn't need the gift, and we could all use humility.

I can't imagine a child without a present to open. How awful would that be? What would it do to a child? I've become more cynical as I've gotten older. I'd like to think that cynicism makes me wiser. On a child, it's a different story.

I've always said that my biggest job as a parent is to keep my kids as innocent as I can for as long as I can. That doesn't mean they need to be sheltered, it just means that they need to be a kid first. Life comes fast enough. Before you know it, you stop believing in Santa, your hormones start racing, you're graduating high school and then one day....BAM! You're setting up the Christmas tree for your kids wondering what happened.

I made the decision to show my son what someone had done. He was just as surprised as I was. We dropped the Bakugon off at a Toys for Tots location. The expression on my son's face said it all. It wasn't easy to give those away.

The entire event has helped me realize how much Christmas means. This Grinch heart grew three sizes that day, if you will. And my son saw how good people really are deep down.

He could only hope Santa would reward him for his kind act in a couple of weeks. I think he will.

And thank you, whoever you are.

(Author's note: I still don't know who you are. I have my suspicions, but no proof. Thanks again.)

Friday Night under the Lights hasn't Changed Much

Little ditty, about Jack and Diane. Or Adam and Robin, for that matter. I was almost scared to send this column in to the paper.

It seems silly now, but I worried about saying "my fiancé", and "our son" in the same column. Unmarried with a child.

Times have changed, and so have I. Now, the step-family seems more the norm than a regular family. Whatever that means.

Of course, I mourn those losses, even as I contribute to them.

That's why I am always cautious about big changes. I like when things like a Friday night football game between two city rivals is still largely the same as when I was a kid.

Styles have changed, and wheeled back around, but the supporting cast is nearly identical, if not down right uncanny.

I know kids are different today, and it's because we are all different. I'm different. But some traditions should just be left alone. Like Friday night, under the lights.

McCune's Manchester

October 30th, 2008

I wish I could get as excited about anything, like the way my 20 month-old son reacts when he sees a balloon.

"Bah-yooon! Bah-yooon!" He'll squeal from his seat in the back of the car when we drive by Autofair and see a trail of balloons on strings flying high up.

You could drop a bag of $100 bills in front of me and my reaction would probably still not match his at the sheer excitement of seeing a helium filled latex balloon.

We walked into Gill Stadium to take in the football game between old city rivals Memorial and Central on Friday. The first thing he spotted was the balloons.

It was Central's homecoming game, and Gill was decorated as such. My poor fiancé is a Memorial alum. Sitting down, we knew what we were in for, both on the field and in the stands. Central was getting ready to cream their opponent on homecoming night, and we were about to spend the night chasing after a child while he explored the spaces of the stadium for a spare balloon.

We irritated the fans in the front row, trying in vain to actually watch the football game. They didn't understand my son's fixation on the balloons.

Some of the fans got a grin watching his sheer joy, others grumbled obscenities under their breath while flashing hot glances our way.

My fiancé started laughing as a group of girls walked by. She couldn't help it, she could have sworn she saw the same style of clothing; tight jeans, ankle boots and big earrings, that were all the rage when she graced these same seats in good humor all those yea....well, let's just say a couple of years ago. Ahem.

It was all there in front of us. Groups of teenagers walking in a close huddle. The girls giggling, the boys posturing and talking loudly. They were all peacocks showing their feathers that night. Like the styles, few things change. Or at least they come back.

I worry about this generation. I worry they'll go too far. I worry what they are headed into and the way they will act when the Time comes. Maybe that means I've finally grown up. There was a time when shaking my head at the idiot behavior of High Schoolers would have been the last thing on my mind. In fact, there was a time not that far removed from today when I was partaking in that same idiot behavior.

All these kids were still taking in a very American moment. Football on a Friday night. Under the lights, marching bands answering each other from either side of the field. Love born and lost in between halftime and the fourth quarter. It was all a very "Mellencamp" moment, only Manchester's version of a "Tasty Freeze", down the street at Cremeland, had already boarded up their windows for the winter.

I'm sure many things happened after we left. I'm sure the gossip from Friday was shared Monday in the halls of Memorial and Central alike. Maybe someone broke up. Maybe that new love was born. Perhaps the girls realized they were wearing the same clothes once worn by their mothers. All of these things made me smile as we left. We scooted out just before halftime, leaving those things behind for the current generation.

The next generation had his balloon to worry about.

Remembering Christ Beste with a Smile

I had a really hard time writing this one. Not because I was close with Chris Beste, but because I wasn't.

Chris Beste was a friendly acquaintance.

We would share a beer or two on occasion, chatting about our similar Midwestern roots. It was a blossoming friendship that I was never able to completely cultivate.

Talking about death is hard enough, but when you send something to be printed off for an entire city to read you had better be careful with what you say.

I received comfort from an unlikely of source, Jim Finnegan, former Union Leader Editorial Page Director He said:

> *I was, and am, deeply moved by your obviously heartfelt tribute to your former comrade in stand-up comedy. I used to dabble in writing at the Union Leader years ago, and I think I know quality writing when I see it.*
>
> *Take a bow and move to the head of the class.*
>
> *- Jim Finnegan*

(Authors note: Dabble? I would say Mr. Finnegan used to do more than dabble...we could all be so modest.)

McCune's Manchester
October 23rd, 2008

I opened the door to the funeral home and it felt like I was walking into a vacuum.

Someone I knew had died. His name was Chris Beste,

and like me, he had tried his hand at stand-up comedy.

For about a year and a half he and I were a part of an open mic night that existed every other Friday at the Bridge Cafe. I recall laughing at his jokes and sharing beers down the street at McGarvey's on more than a few of those nights after we would wrap up.

He had a stage presence that stuck in my mind.

He would rock back and forth, like a clock ticking down to the punchline. Clutching the microphone tight to his face, his low voice would boom over the crowd. Delivering the punchline, his face would glow with a sly smile. He would stare off towards the back counter, trying not to laugh at his own joke as he lowered the microphone waiting for the laughter to subside.

That's how I remembered him, as I walked into the funeral home. Today, there were no smiles inside. That vacuum was stifling.

I never know quite how I should act when I'm in those circumstances. Sitting down, I looked at his body. It haunted the room. His family was grieving over the loss. He was just 30 years old.

Like many comedians trying to work their way through the ranks of smoky rooms, cafes, Asian restaurants and back rooms of bars, he held a day job. He was a union carpenter. If you heard about the story last week, you know Chris died as the result of an accident.

Watching the friends and family of Chris forced me to think of my own mortality. Who would come to my funeral? Obviously, these are never happy occasions. Still, the little reunions are nice to see, even if they are under such awful circumstance.

I met up with two other comedians from those days at the Bridge Cafe. One I hadn't seen in quite some time. We talked and soon our blank expressions turned to smiles. We were laughing, trying to remember him the way we should.

That's how I want to go. I know that a funeral exists mostly for those that are left. But when I go, I want people to laugh and remember the good times. I grew up with Irish-Catholic roots, and it shows when someone I know passes. There's the mourning phase and there is the immediate phase that exists soon after the wake or funeral. That's the phase where everyone crawls to the nearest bar and lifts a glass in toast to a life, remembering they are now in a better place.

By the time I left the funeral home, the vacuum I felt coming in had been replaced by warm thoughts and funny memories. We strained to remember the jokes of a man that we all felt was funny, and in the end shared a laugh over his unique style and presence.

For someone that I new only on a week-to-week basis, it seemed like a huge void had left. I smiled as I found out something I never knew about him, that he was a huge supporter of the Special Olympics. I walked out feeling an odd sense of peace.

The world was a little less funny today, but at least his memories will live on. Now if I could just remember some of his jokes.

WZID's Bronson is off to Big Apple

Bob's been doing well since this column came out. Still rocking the Big Apple. Don't worry, I'm sure being in Yankees/Mets/Jets/Giants land it isn't too hard for him...he was a Dolphins fan anyway.

McCune's Manchester
May 7th, 2009

It's a hot July day in 1987. A group of friends from Boston drive up to see Tom Petty play on the asphalt in Arms Park in Manchester.

"This is my first parking lot concert," one of them says. He's a young man, with a handsome face and the definitive Italian look. The group was in for it.

"Where's the concert?" One of the men in the group asks, as it dawns on them they will spend the concert melting into the asphalt.

The summer heat was particularly brutal on that day, and the parking-lot-concert-virgins were about to be baked in it. They parked under the bridge and headed in for a sweltering concert.

Manchester was a very different city in those days. The Millyard looked a little barren. There were no sports franchises. And national bands coming through town were forced to play in parking lots.

"It's kind of a downtrodden town," the man says. And in some ways, it's true. It will be a few years before the city sees its eventual rebirth. This is well before the Arena, the Fisher Cats, WiFi, or texting. This is a time where rock and roll was still recorded on tape. Most people still had a record player, and Tom Petty was cranking out the hits.

Flash-forward 16 years and one of the guys from that group who took in the Tom Petty concert returned to park his car near that same lot. It was a very different day, a cold December day. Bob Bronson had come back, but not for another concert. This time he was there to take the reins as the Program Director of WZID, and eventually the afternoon slot on the station.

Full disclosure here, Bob was my boss while I held down that same afternoon shift on WZID. I remember my first encounter with him, at the Manchester Airport. He was looking at a newspaper carefully peering over the top, waiting to pick me up for my interview.

Last week, Bob said his goodbyes to listeners as he headed off into the sunset. He's not retiring, he's headed towards greener pastures.

Bob Bronson will be part of the morning show on WLTW in New York City. Hitting it big in the Big Apple is an accomplishment itself, but Bob happens to be moving to the number one station in the number one market in the country.

To put it on another local term, it's like one of the Fisher Cats pitchers being called up to be the ace of the Blue Jays. It's a huge deal, and it rarely happens like that in radio, at least not anymore.

That same guy who had watched Tom Petty on a scorching hot parking lot in Manchester saw a very different city when he arrived in 2003. Manchester had just experienced its new Renaissance. Fresh off of a few "Best Places to Live" lists, the city added the Verizon Wireless Arena, two "major" minor-league sports franchises, not to mention the re-purposed real estate

WZID's offices occupy in the millyard. Everything had turned around.

I try to picture that first moment he walked into his new office and looked down at the river and parking lot and thought of that concert he saw when he was 16 years younger. What a different view it must have been.

So last week, when Bob said goodbye, it was bittersweet for me. I'm genuinely happy for him, but sad to see him go. In some ways, Bob was a father figure to me in his tenure at the station. I always felt as though he had my back, and gave me guidance when I needed it.

I asked him if the transition was tough to sell to his family.

"They understand it's a big market, and a big opportunity," continuing with, "she did marry a radio guy." He was talking about his wife Carolyn. His three daughters were sold on the idea as soon as they heard Britney Spears spent some time with the morning show just a month ago.

Still, he said it was a hard decision to make. He leaves behind a radio station that can, at times, seem like a family, but he said he leaves no regrets.

Next time he comes through Manchester, the city will look different again. He'll see it with new eyes, New York City eyes. He just promises not to be wearing a Yankees hat when he returns to visit.

And if he returns for a Tom Petty concert, I'm sure it won't be on the asphalt, it will be at the Verizon Wireless Arena.

It's Time We Start Trusting Each Other

Sadly, I'm still guilty of some of these habits that lead to not trusting anyone anymore. Some of that is the safety of common sense. Still, a majority of that feeling is just being resistant to that change.

McCune's Manchester
May 7th, 2009

Trust.

We don't have it anymore. As we close out another year and another decade, ultimately, the lack of trust we have for each other defines those measures of time.

Case in point:

In 1998, I was driving my car along a back country road when I ran out of gas. Blame it on youthful ignorance or just plain being bold enough to think I wouldn't run out of gas, but there I sat on the side of the road. I got out and started to hoof it to a nearby gas station. Soon, a car came by and the complete stranger offered me a ride. When I came to the gas station, the person working there gave me the loaner can, and a gallon of gas as my stranger-driver gave me a lift back to my abandoned car...which I had left unlocked without a thought.

Now, a similar moment happened just a few weeks ago to me, except this time, I was on the way to drop off my son at school. Again, the car herked and jerked until I came to a stop and realized what had happened; I was out of fuel.

So, I walked with my two sons to school on that slushy morning, and then to a gas station with my two-year-old to grab a loaner can and get going on my way.

The clerk gave me a confused look when I asked about a loaner can. She had never heard of such a thing. Has it really been a long enough span of time that this idea has become some ancient relic of years gone by?

I started walking back home to grab my own can out of the shed, and thought about how things have changed.

I used to pull up to a gas station, fill the tank, and walk in to pay the cashier. This practice is now completely gone. If I decide to even use cash, I must first go inside and decide how much I intend to buy. The usual manner is to swipe your card, and trust that there is enough money in your bank account to cover that tank of fuel.

And what about bathrooms? How many gas station bathrooms have suddenly become off limits in the past decade? First, you had to sheepishly ask the attendant for a key. Then, they started attaching giant objects to the keys, because apparently someone started stealing the keys so they could have their own executive bathroom at Cumby's.

Now, I've noticed a lot of convenience stores have closed up the bathroom entirely. How convenient.

I don't claim innocence in the trust department. I'm just as guilty as everyone else.

I make judgments on people as they stand in line in front of me in the grocery store. I decide if they are trustworthy or not, simply by appearance. Then, get indignant when I see those same looks coming back at me.

On Tuesday, I got a call from my bank. It seems I had

left my checkbook at the Target in Bedford. I only use my checkbook to pay bills, so I was instantly suspicious.

On the surface, I was blown away that someone cared enough to find it, hand it to a clerk, and they actually took the time to call my bank instead of throwing it away. But in the back of my head, I envisioned a large check clearing my narrow account.

I logged into my account online and balanced my checking account. It was normal, and I felt strangely awful. Not only had no one stole my checkbook, to go on a Target shopping spree, they had been trustworthy enough to turn it in anonymously.

When I went to pick it up, the store had a system of checks and measures to ensure that my checkbook had been kept in a quiet place, locked away, where only a handful of people knew of its existence. They didn't even trust most of their employees to even allow them to know where it was kept.

I guess if we are to start trusting people again, it starts with each of us. Not only do we have to open our minds to the idea that people can be trusted, we have to stop doing things that void that trust. The obvious reason we stopped trusting people is that we are paying attention, and people do bad things.

So I say good riddance to 2009, and good riddance to the first decade of this century. Let's bring on the next year and the next decade, I'm ready to start trusting people again.

Places

Home Like a Date Until Time to Part

The pitfalls of homeownership should be brought up in Home Economics classes in high school. Not once did anyone ever warn me that the boiler will go out the same time your toilet is overflowing, or your lawn is so lumpy that you will wear out a lawnmower every year, or that your house somehow knows you have an extra $2,000 in your savings account, so something major is about to die and swallow all of that money immediately.

Nope. No one ever said that to me. But that is exactly how it works.

When we first listed our house, the housing bubble had yet to pop. This column was about the second time we listed the house, almost two years after our first attempt.

By this time, we had another child and added a dog. Our house is meant to be a starter home; perfect for young couples and single people, but not for a family of four with cats and dogs running all over the place.

Leaving the house is a lot like a breakup of a relationship, and the process of finding a new home is so much like the dating game. The balance struck me as odd. So I wrote about it.

McCune's Manchester
January 28th, 2010

Finding the right house is a courtship. The perils, rewards and heartache are on par with the typical dating ritual, and the end results are not that different.

Take us, for example. In the traditional sense, I guess

we are trying to trade up our house. Of course, this is exactly what most people do in the dating world. They stay with someone long enough, because they are comfortable, safe, and at least surface-level happy.

Then, a big promotion, or a life changing moment comes along and things change. Suddenly, you need something more suitable for your conditions. A little more space, a facade that is more appealing.

You try out a new house, much like a date. You see them for the first time, check them out, ask the right questions, hopefully getting the right answers, and in the end if there is something you don't like, you simply say to your friends, "I can change it. It's not that difficult, I've done it before." And you do.

Hopefully, the end result isn't a messy divorce. I guess on the housing level, divorce is equivalent to foreclosure. You leave, perhaps sooner than you had hoped, and in the end, you end up with nothing, or less than nothing, wondering why it happened to you.

I see a lot of these house-divorces on our searches. And I see the trial separations too, the short-sales, where people try to get out from under the housing bubble and escape with their finances intact. They have to leave their washer and dryer behind, not even able to visit on the weekends.

It isn't easy. We've escaped it a couple of times ourselves. And there is a certain dread you feel when the end of your house-relationship might be near.

For us, and our house, it is an amicable split. We've decided to part our ways. We need more space, and the house is finally tired of the animals clicking around on its floor.

Our house would prefer a new couple, a younger couple, and we don't blame it. Our needs have changed too. You see house, it's not you, it's us. Two bedrooms is simply too few for four people, two dogs and three cats to share. We will miss you. And we want you to have that washer and dryer, and the new stove we bought. It's okay, you enjoy them with your new couple; your young couple. We just want you to be happy.

This courtship is so brutal, and harsh that we need other people to facilitate it. We look at pictures online and scour descriptions, trying to find imperfections and flaws in between the sentences.

We pay these people to sit through this process with us. They are well-mannered, well adjusted, and smile as you look at houses that are all wrong for you. Then, they pull you aside, and tell you that you are making a grave mistake.

"The wiring is all wrong with this one," they say. And it's true! But you've fallen in love with every other part, that your trying to look past the crazy things that happen, and weird electrical demons. But in the end, it is always best to listen to these people.

And for those that fear all of these horrible, awful pitfalls of the housing relationship, there is a last hope. You can avoid all of these problems of the housing relationship and stay in an apartment. But those people are just afraid of commitment.

Starting a Fitness Regimen Hurts Less than Laser Tag

My Doctor never told me to play laser tag three times a day, but it would be a perfect exercise. It's strenuous, uses all of your muscles, and your brain, and has an almost sick rewarding side to it when you shoot a six year old at point-blank range. So what if he's the birthday boy? He probably deserved it.

McCune's Manchester
January 14th, 2010

We did it. We joined the YMCA. There is no turning back.

The lure of an indoor area to swim, workout, and rock climb was a bit too powerful. A place to watch the kids while we accomplish all of this was the kicker. It was the pull of this attraction that led me to overdo it the first day I started.

We brought the family into the Allard Center in Goffstown, and split up to our destinations. I worked out, hopping on a stationary bike and several free-weight machines before going to the rock-climbing wall, then swimming ten laps in the pool, and finally a good 15 minute soak in the steam shower.

It was about three hours later when it hit me...I overdid it. I started feeling very tired, my stomach hurt and I just had that overall malaise of not-feeling-good.

Then I remembered; this is what it feels like to exercise. Still, the next day, I felt pretty good. At the very least, my wife and I were continuing on our goal of getting in shape in the new year. Don't call it a resolution, because those have a habit of failing. Call it a promise to each other.

In my day-after glow, I brought my son to a birthday party at Space Center in Hooksett. This is when I hit The Wall.

In all of my excitement, of exercising and feeling good about myself, I was safe and stretched out before and after my workout. All was good. But in the rush to swoop into the laser-tag area, and arm ourselves against a band of four teenagers, who used the names of South Park characters as their own, I somehow forgot to stretch. Big mistake.

It was all well and good for 45 minutes inside the frozen, 5,000 square foot palace of laser tag heaven. We blasted and shot our way through four games, trying in vain to lead a group of six and seven year olds against those teenagers. In the end, I have to admit that the teenagers won...handily. The score of the Patriots playoff game was closer.

Still, it was fun. More fun than a 31 year old should have playing with kids. It was a little intense, in fact. There were genuine moments of fear and victory, the rush of adrenaline and the agony of defeat. I guess that is why I shouldn't have been surprised on Monday morning when I woke up and felt like I had played on the losing end in that Pats game.

Every muscle in my body ached, especially my legs. Apparently, it wasn't just the teenagers that kicked my butt, it was the course itself. The act of crouching to avoid imaginary enemy fire had produced a pounding feeling in my thighs. What was this strange sensation? I could actually feel the definition of my legs, without touching them.

Casually, and very coyly, I bowed out of a planned trip back to the Y the next day. It was simply too much. If there is anything I learned in this process, I guess it is that I need to know when to say when.

The next day, my muscles were a little less sore, and my mind was back in it. Time to get back exercising, because you never know when you'll have to play laser tag with six year olds again.

Sometimes Dreams Don't Turn out Well

One tiny thing that stands out about this column is the last paragraph. I tried to gracefully tip-toe around what I was really saying; that the bull statue has a pair of testicles.

I'm still amused by this, because there has to be a logic structure as to why the bull is anatomically correct.

I guess if you are a sculptor, you are probably a purist in the sense that you want things to be exactly as they are. So a part of me thinks the bull's "correct" underside is because the artist wanted it that way.

On the other hand, the statue represents the old Jac-Pac meat packing factory that was near where the Hands Across the Merrimack Bridge sits on the river's east bank. So perhaps the former workers would have been so upset that the artist was afraid omitting the testicles would be seen as an artistic statement and fears of retaliation, in its most gruesome forms, went through his head.

The positioning of the statue is also questionable. Why not have the bull face people as they enter and exit to the bridge's downtown side? Why on Earth would you give people the "business end" view of the statue?

This column was an exercise in restraint. It was very hard to say what I wanted without offending readers with my blunt language.

Still, as you will see in the column that follows, I was the one that ended up getting the business end when some readers challenged me to do something more than just complain about how it looks.

**McCune's Manchester
October 15th, 2009**

It's a shame when a bad thing happens to a good idea.

That is exactly what has happened to the Hands Across the Merrimack Bridge.

The project was a success after its completion more than a year ago. The gaping expanse from just south of Merchantsauto.com stadium to the city's West side was blighted by the old bridge. It was a palette for taggers and an eyesore for the city.

So I was one of the first to cheer when they decided to finally restore the bridge and use it for walking and bikers. It made sense. That is how good things happen, people get concerned, see an idea and give birth to a wonderful new addition to the city.

We haven't done a good job maintaining that bridge.

I took my son for a walk down there a few weeks ago, and was disgusted with what I saw. I pulled up and looked at the weeds, overgrown worse than our neglected lawn at home. I shrugged it off as just an oversight, the type of thing that will eventually cure itself through the help of those who were behind the project to begin with.

When I pushed the stroller along the parking lot on the West Side that abuts the trail and bridge, I was dismayed to find that this has become somewhat of a new dump for people unloading television sets that are no longer useful in the age of HDTVs. That wasn't all. Computer monitors, an arm chair and several mattresses lined the walk up the hill to the entrance of the bridge.

How quickly the place has turned, I thought.

Walking over the bridge, I tried to forget about the garbage and take in the city's skyline. I looked down at the cold water of the Merrimack and discovered more signs of abuse. It was a bicycle. A bike, in the water, obviously flung off the side of the bridge. My natural instinct was to blame it on kids, perhaps someone playing a prank. But then I noticed another bike. Then a shopping cart, about a half dozen tires and even another television set.

What happened? What was once a beautiful dream was now becoming a dark dumping ground for someone. What a shame.

Years were spent trying to raise the funds for this bridge project. A community came together and built a walking bridge, uniting two neighborhoods and spawning an inter-city trail system that now includes Goffstown's Rail Trail. This project was years in the making, costing piles of money raised by hard working people and this is what we do with it?

I don't know how you go about stopping people from

dumping things off the side. I still like to think that would be the work of kids just being stupid. Hopefully, whoever it is, grows out of this behavior.

The hidden nature of the back side street near the parking lot area on the West Side gives people too much cover right now to dump their trash. I think there needs to be another light around this area to deter people from dumping. And the overgrown weeds provide cover for people trying to dump off their refuse.

I pushed my son to the other side of the bridge, disgusted with the sights that I had seen. We were greeted by the bull statue put in place near the end of the summer.

The placement of the bull seemed somewhat fitting, given the circumstances. The bull faces downtown, giving those that pass by what a butcher might refer to as the "business end" of the animal. I chuckled, turning the stroller back the other way and towards our car, parked in the dump/parking lot on the other side.

I guess you could call it a fitting monument to what started as a beautiful idea.

Putting Your Money Where Your Mouth Is

Boy, I sure did. I have to give a big thanks to Steve, Ed and my mother-in-law. They helped quite a bit.

A little bit of back-story; the lot we actually cleaned up is private property. We had no idea. When I found this out later, I called the owner to tell him what we did. Let's just say he was not too pleased. He was very worried this would be negative attention.

I suggested that part of his property near this lot could be used as a community garden. He went through the roof, taking my suggestion as a slight against him personally.

To be honest, I meant no harm. Now, if you go there, they have taken excellent care of the land. Being a landlord is hard work, and taking care of space that isn't actively occupied by tenants is probably the last thing anyone in that scenario wants to deal with.

I also realized the error of my ways when I found out you should call the city weeks ahead of time for such an extensive clean up. Luckily, they understood the massive eye-sore that would be there if for that long and were able to squeeze in a pick up. They deserve a huge thanks in this.

My other fault was that I decided to clean up during a Patriots game. That cut my potential workforce by serious numbers. I really didn't consider it, because I am a Packer fan. I make no apologies for that.

Basically, I learned my lesson. Helping out means doing your homework. You have to know what you're doing, where you're doing it and who will be effected by what you are doing. Consulting an NFL schedule doesn't hurt, either.

In the end, the property was cleaned up, if only temporarily, and I still maintain that we did a good thing.

McCune's Manchester
November 12th, 2009

Sometimes, you just have to put your money where your mouth is. It's a cliche statement, for sure, but it makes sense.

In my case, it came true.

About a month ago, I wrote about the Hands Across the Merrimack Bridge, and how the area was blighted by trash in all forms. Weeds, garbage, couches, televisions, you name it.

One reader called me on it, saying "If you decide on your own to go over there and collect some of that trash, let me know."

In fact, several readers said they would be interested in helping with a clean-up. Suddenly, I was deputized as an organizer, which admittedly, isn't my strongest suit.

On Sunday, we gathered. The group was much smaller than I had hoped, helped in part by my decision to start at 1:00pm, the exact time of the Patriots game. The group consisted of myself, Steve Gamlin, Ed Gawrys and my mother-in-law, Lorie. Quite the group. Steve brought a dolly, and went to work in the weeds near the highway, quickly pulling out several items. Steve was also trying to put his money where his mouth is. He's a motivational speaker, who tells people that if they see an opportunity to do some quick volunteering, to do it. Steve was doing his.

I started clearing the weeds along the road, which were a good six to eight feet high, providing too much cover for people to throw trash. Ed and Lorie went to work clearing dead weeds and picking up trash.

We worked for a little over and hour, clearing, picking and hauling. In the end, we found a mountain of garbage in those weeds. The size of it was shameful.

There was a couch, two arm chairs, a set of four tires, three television sets, a couple of computer monitors, and four or five bags of garbage. Pretty much an entire furnished living room was found in those weeds.

In picking up the trash, we came across all sorts of interesting things. There were dirty diapers, bottles of vodka wrapped in paper bags, dozens of empty soda bottles, and a pile of empty packages of ephedrine, which can be used in the manufacturing of methamphetamine. It was scary.

While we were cleaning, I saw a family walking on the bridge, pushing something. Soon, they came down and thanked us for cleaning up. I had this nagging feeling and walked up the steps to the bridge. I found what they were pushing...a shopping cart. We added it to the garbage pile.

We finished up, snapped a couple of pictures, and were ready to leave when one resident came and talked to us. At first, I thought he might come out to thank us. Instead, he told us about what is happening in his neighborhood.

Every night, scores of teenagers come to the parking lot, playing loud music, drinking and doing other things in the cars. This resident said he calls the cops, but the police are, ironically, hand-cuffed to do much about it until someone witnesses someone committing a crime. The brush and lack of lighting provide cover for these activities. Our friend feels like he is out of options, and even fears retaliation.

I thought the worst problem was the pile of garbage we hauled out of the woods and brush. That wasn't the case at all.

Again, the catalyst for this was simply a problem area in need of help. The bridge is supposed to connect the city's West Side to the main arteries, not connect from the East bank of the river and then be forgotten in blight and trash.

If the problem isn't fixed, it will only get worse. At the very least, there needs to be better lighting and at least one or two trash cans. Those two things, along with upkeep of the weeds would keep at least some of the garbage in check, and keep the lot from becoming Manchester's West Side landfill. Those are only band-aids to the larger root problems, for which I have no answer.

All I can say is that if you see a problem, and you can help fix it, do it. There are steps you have to take along the way, like calling the Manchester Highway Department ahead of time to schedule a trash pick-up, and work around their schedule. I challenge anyone in the city to give an hour of their time to doing just that. If we all did that, Manchester would be New Hampshire's most beautiful city.

It Was More Fun in Costumes on Oct. 31

When I e-mailed this column to my editor, John Toole, he immediately called me back.

It seems that Joe McQuaid was going to publish a similar column.

This put me in a difficult place. Do we decide to re-write the column and try a different idea? I was limited in time, so this was going to be difficult. Or perhaps we should just roll with it and publish the thing.

In the end, we decided to go for it and publish the

piece. I realized that Mr. McQuaid and I might have a different audience, even in the same paper. People who look for his editorials may not be the same people who look for my column.

I take comfort in the fact that Joe McQuaid and I came to the same conclusion, even though our backgrounds are entirely different. That common ground means a lot to me.

McCune's Manchester
October 22nd, 2009

I know I'm going to sound like an old man. But Halloween ain't what it used to be.

Somewhere between the time I was a kid and when my two boys starting enjoying this holiday, something happened.

Maybe I'm finally old. Perhaps this is part of becoming an adult. Maybe, just maybe, I'm a curmudgeon at heart.

Let me start this old-person rant:

When I was kid, Halloween used to be Halloween. And I mean, ON Halloween. None of this "2-4pm", daylight only, make sure your safe, don't take candy from strangers non-sense that we have today. We trick-or-treated on October 31st. It didn't matter what the weather was. In fact, I have a very distinct memory of doing just that during the middle of a freak 36-inch Wisconsin snow storm. I tumbled around in the back seat of our Buick (probably without a seatbelt) as we drifted from house to house in search of the Big Score.

This is back when the playground slides didn't have

bumpers, everything gave you a sliver, and nothing seemed like a big deal.

My costumes weren't elaborate. In fact, they were pretty run-of-the-mill. Put a bandanna on my head, slap on an eye patch, a little of mom's mascara for a beard and I was a pirate. End of story.

Now, parents aren't doing the right thing unless they pay $40 to get the latest movie character costume. The material for these costumes is lighter than the stuff they use to make generic trash bags - without the drawstring, and the designs barely resemble the characters they are supposed to be.

That is why I'm thankful for my mother. She has always been an expert seamstress.

Last year, my mother sewed a costume for my oldest son. It was "Spider Monkey", a bit character on one of his favorite shows at the time; Ben 10 Alien Force.

I was unsure. The character wasn't the main guy. Besides, I thought, Spider Monkey has four arms and a tail. In my role as the current-day parent, I only want the best costume for my kids. I know what a big deal it is to them, in spite of my old-man ways.

My son, though, was very excited. When the costume arrived and he wore it to school, it was an instant hit. While parents scratched their heads and wondered what in the world this four armed beast really was, the kids understood immediately.

Naturally, this year, we turned to grandma again. This time, the character is "Dan" from the ever-popular Bakugan. Don't ask, I still don't know what that means. Grandma got her sewing machine out and went to work.

My other son decided he was going to get into the

madness. He asked to be a moose. Not just any moose, a purple moose. My wife has decided to take a nod from my mother and sew it herself.

The first order of business was to talk him into a brown moose, instead of his fancy purple color. There was something about explaining why he was purple at least a dozen times over that was very unappealing to us.

Still, I'm a traditionalist at heart.

Remember that as you take your kids out trick-or-treating this Sunday between the hours of 1 and 4 pm. in Manchester (yes, during the Patriots game...again.) Think about how it used to be. Tell your kids, let them know. Maybe they'll appreciate that soon-to-be-outdated Monsters vs. Aliens costume a little bit more.

A Corral at the Mall Rounds 'em Up

Oh, this place. I have a love/hate relationship with the corral at the mall. The kids love going there, I loathe dealing with the parents of the other kids that frequent the same spot. I wrote this column after my first trip to the corral.

Since then, I've decided to make myself scarce on that real estate. In reality, and I stress this point, it isn't the kids, it's the parents. And it certainly isn't the mall. They put in a nice thing that people have done their best to ruin.

Awful parents that toss their kids in the "corral" only to stroll out and sit outside of the boundary and sip on a soda, while texting on their phone.

It clearly states that children must be accompanied by an adult. That doesn't matter to these people, who do nothing, in fact don't even notice that little Jimmy is tearing some kid's hair out. I wonder if they would care if they saw it.

People like that make my blood boil.

McCune's Manchester
February 12th, 2009

Parents are always looking for that quiet place to grab a couple of moments for themselves. While I can't promise it will be totally quiet, I can promise the new play area at the Mall of New Hampshire is enough of a distraction to let you escape to your own thoughts, if only for that brief moment.

We stumbled on the new area, a soft-tumble faux barnyard set up in the rotunda of the food court, on a recent mall trip. We've been back again and again.

Basically, it's a corral with one opening. Inside the half-height walls, set up in a circle, there is a giant barn in the middle (complete with a pesky real life bird who keeps thinking he's outside), a tractor, a cow, a slide and a plastic bale of hay.

I have to admit, I chuckled when I saw the plastic hay. It was so smooth and shiny, I did a double take, wondering what it was that I just saw.

The kids run around like mad men and women. The hierarchy they pretend now usually becomes the real deal as they get older.

I've watched my kids play with much interest, carefully keeping track of how they interact with each other. The bully now, is sure to be either the criminal or CEO later in life. Maybe both.

Neither of my kids appear to have those traits, thankfully. It's how they deal with that bully that's important to me.

My five year old just ignores him, and comes over to me to tell all about it. Perhaps he'll be a whistle blower someday. I have mixed emotions about that. My two year old just stares at those bully kids and finally laughs before running away. This is the perfect reaction. He'll be the guy who just doesn't let things get to him. Don't sweat the small stuff.

About every five minutes one kid tries to make a break for it. The one opening shows the wonder of the rest of the mall. The temptation is just too much. You can actually watch the kids forming the plan in their mind. They look at the opening. Then they stare. Three seconds later, they are at a full sprint. One parent usually catches up to them before they hit the Orange Julius stand. But every now and then, they make it all the way to Blake's.

We were there on a recent Saturday when some kid was running around with the steering wheel from the tractor. It was complete madness. The kids were running around, screaming in a wild pack that made me think I was witnessing Lord of the Flies coming to life. Who was in charge here? Was it the parents, or was it the kids?

The parents, and to be frank, it's mostly mothers, sit around sipping their Dunkin Donuts with extra-extra like each touch of the coffee was an old Calgon Soap commercial.

"Oh, Dunkin Donuts, take me away!"

Most of the parents do this as scoff laws. The rules strictly prohibit food and drink of any kind. Strollers are also a no-no, along with shoes. I've seen a few mothers chase after their offspring while they were wearing heels. It's a comical sight, as the bottom is layered with a padding, giving the kids the added cushion should they fall. The result is a mother stumbling after her child while the kid laugh at mom's strange wobbly walk.

Sure is different than my day. First, we didn't really have many indoor play areas when I was a child. That was a technology reserved for McDonald's communicable disease ball pits. We've come a long way. Otherwise, playgrounds were strictly outside only. Kids of my generation and before were treated to the luxury of a playground only during the warmer months. And there was no safety to speak of. There was what seemed like a ten foot drop off the swing, usually ending with children leaping off. This resulted in about a 15% broken arm ratio.

The slides seemed to stretch a mile into the air and were baked by the hot summer sun. Touching them with your hand was out of the question. But we were expected to slide down, with bare legs poking through our shorts, and make it to the end without a third degree burn. I'm still not sure how I managed to stay out of the emergency room when I was a kid.

The mall corral is a nice respite from our awful rotten winter. It's inside, it's warm. The kids love it and the parents get a much-needed break before rounding up their brood, strapping them into their five point harness and driving back home, off into the sunset.

What's in a Name?

I still think it was silly money to throw at something like this. $100,000! The sign has a light that changes colors around it. How silly is that?

This is a problem of allocation. This money was allocated for this monstrosity, and by golly, that's what it is going to go for!

And the name, "Rimmon Heights" makes the neighborhood sound like a slum. I understand the historical significance, but to an outsider, it's a giant sign that does nothing but mock the inhabitants of the neighborhood it sits in.

McCune's Manchester
May 29th, 2008

What would you do with $100,000?

Currently, it would be advised that you start some sort of home-brew oil refinery, but maybe that's out of the question.

What does the city do with $100,000? They erect three iron arches.

Wonderful!

I can almost hear the phone calls to city hall:

Hello, City Hall. What? Oh, you wanted a police presence on Kelley Street? Well, sir, you'll have one. You see, we are posting uniformed guards on 24 hour watches to secure our new sign posts, proclaiming your neighborhood as "Rimmon Heights." It seems like a bit much, but we don't want anything to happened to those signs...Those things are expensive.

What's Rimmon Heights? That's the neighborhood surrounding Kelley Street. I think they got the name from an episode of the television show "Cops." Hello? Hello, sir? He hung up on me!

What sounds better, telling people you live on Kelley Street or in Rimmon Heights? It doesn't even have the ring that "Pinardville" has, does it?

It's a nice effort, and yes, it's good that the city is finally paying attention to the West Side. But was this the right move? Aren't the people in this neighborhood screaming for safety? Unless the new signs create some sort of force field, I don't think they will help.

A bit flippant maybe. But when the residents are asking for more police presence, isn't it silly to give them a sign with a name on it that they never heard of?

This is a case of misplaced good will. An area rarely transforms with a forced renaissance. The "Rimmon Heights" neighborhood is the first area of the city to see assistance from a vague sweeping plan for renewal. Call it "economic stimulus" before it was cool. The idea was set into motion in January of last year, well before our biggest worry was how to pay for gasoline and bread. I understand something has to be done, but maybe it's time to put a few of these projects on hold while we figure out where the city and its residents are at financially.

When the city announced their plans back in January of 2007, St. Mary's Bank starting offering reduced rates for those trying to fix up homes in the neighborhood. It's a step in the right direction. Though I wonder if some of the absentee owners of those triple deckers took advantage of that. I think those absentee owners are part of the problem around Kelley Street, I mean "Rimmon Heights."

What the city is doing amounts to putting lipstick on a pig. In the end, it's still a pig and no one has done anything about the fact that they don't like pork. And the fact is, a little new blacktop, an iron sign and a new coat of paint on a couple of triple deckers doesn't amount to "improvements" in my book.

For a real urban renaissance to take place, the citizens that live in "Rimmon Heights" have to bring it on. There has been a start. A Pizza place, a 99 cent store, even a jeweler are recent commercial additions. All of those businesses came before the signpost. Bob and Sons repair has been there for years, and continues to shine. Chiggy's always seems to be busy. There is hope for the rest of the neighborhood.

More police, better roads, repaired sidewalks. Those are basic things that the people in that neighborhood need. Maybe they can sell the signs for scrap and pay for one of them.

There's Light at the End of the Bridge

I think I must have went through a span where I was angry about everything. I admit, I love being able to go North on 293, and the benefit to businesses is probably a great thing, but it was another project that seems like it cost too much.

McCune's Manchester

June 19th, 2008

Ahhhhh. To turn right and go North from the Granite Street Bridge.

Is it possible? Am I dreaming?

My five year old son doesn't remember a time when the Granite street bridge wasn't under construction. My second child was conceived, born and is now walking and talking, all in the span of the renovation on the bridge.

Every trip across that bridge has been more bewildering than the last. Changing traffic patterns, rabid drivers, new blacktop, strange contraptions moving awkwardly into place, surly police officers dutifully burning in the sun. What a place that bridge has been.

And it's all in the name of progress. God, I hope it's worth it. Every morning, I've crossed that bridge around 5 am. And every morning, every single light turns red as I approach. Without fail, I've hit every red light on my solitary trip. All for the right to make a right turn.

Well I suppose that's not the only reason. The bridge was in terrible shape. There's also a 293 South Exit 5 we have. That will make it much easier to explain directions to the Verizon or Merchantsauto.com stadium to people from Concord and points North.

I know I'm not alone in my hatred of this construction. I've seen you on the bridge. Blank stares, hollow expressions, droning off to the constant sucking sound of the carburetor or fuel injector eating away at your summer vacation.

We all have sawed off tempers on that bridge. I've tossed a few four-letter words at fellow drivers myself.

Who wouldn't be mad? Here we are, stuck together, just wanting to move, $4 a gallon at a time and for what? To turn right.

I suppose those stuck on 293 South have had similar thoughts. Bumper to bumper, door to door, temper to temper with the other drivers. All in pursuit of their jobs and offices to the South. But hey, if Frankie Foxx tells you there is an accident on 293 between Exits 4 and 5...well now you can swing off the exit, onto Second Street and into the inevitable jam of cars trying to escape into Exit 4's oblivion.

Isn't progress a great thing?

There are a lot of positives about the new Bridge.

The new blacktop is nice. The sidewalks are wide and new. The extra lanes will be helpful for the concerts and games in town. It really is a sign of how lucky we are in Manchester.

Think about it. Minor League Baseball, Minor League Hockey, Arena Football all in one city, and all without wasting precious gasoline. Elton John, Van Halen, even Aerosmith (let's hope they get well and swing back through...) all right here. Manchester is what a lot of cities strive to be.

So a couple of years of cussing and honking and burning and sucking on the tailpipe of the car in front of you is worth it. And that right turn onto 293 is probably the sweetest right turn you can make, if only it means an end to the construction.

Use a Fresh Pair of Eyes

You never know who you are going to make angry.

People are apparently very attached to River Road. I was flooded with e-mails after this column came out that there was "no such thing as 'North' River Road"

I have lived for 22 years on what USED TO BE called North River Road in Manchester. About 10 years ago, the Postal Service left letters in mailboxes for the many of us on this long road saying that the fire and police depts. decided to change the name to just River Rd. because having North in it was too confusing for emergency personnel.

The letter said everyone had to accept this and to change all pre-addressed stationery, notify friends, family, bills, (and) magazines by a certain date or they would stop delivering mail to us.

Also at that time all street signs were changed to show only *River Rd.*

This had been NORTH River Rd. since the beginnings of *Manchester almost two hundred years ago but we had no choice and the change seemed for a good cause.*

So I don't understand why the Union Leader still uses North in all articles having to do with River Rd.

A couple weeks ago in an article about Stark Park, it was said to be on NORTH River Rd.

Yesterday, there was a picture of geese crossing River Rd. but the caption said NORTH River Rd.

Last week, in Adam McCune's 8/14 column, he talked of taking a car ride from the Amoskeag Bridge to Hooksett with "a fresh pair of eyes" but called this

NORTH River Rd. a couple times. Or maybe Mr. McCune submitted the article to (the) editors with River Rd. in it since he must've seen the over two dozen street signs along the way, and the editors changed it to North when going to print?

I miss the old NORTH River Rd. and know there are more important things in this world to worry about but *the* change was long ago and shouldn't our local newspaper call local streets by their correct names? The editors should do as the many of us who live on River Rd. reluctantly had *to* do .... finally accept the change, stop perpetuating confusion, and correct the name to River Rd. Or maybe they'd like it if everyone kept calling the New Hampshire Union Leader the Manchester Union as it was named many years ago?

- Cheryl

And my response:

Wow.

Apparently, I struck a nerve. I understand your frustration, but you have to understand colloquialism. If *I* called it "River Road" people who didn't live there would think about Bedford, not North Manchester. Go to google maps. Look around at Manchester, nearly every major thoroughfare has about 3 or 4 different *names,* it's confusing to outsiders, but we just grin and bear it. If I were to go strictly by post office designation, there is *no* "Mast Road", it's Route 114. And "Pinardville" doesn't exist. For that matter, Pinardville is a part of

*Manchester, not Goffstown, as the zip code is 03102.
 But that's only because there is no Goffstown Post Office
near there, only a Manchester Annex...So the Post Office
isn't always the be-all, end-all.
The point of the column was not to call attention to*
North *vs Just River Road, but to point out what a strange cross-
section the road is. The Union Leader is pretty good about
printing opposing viewpoints in the opinion section, so I
wouldn't be surprised if they printed it.*

*Have a better day, I think of your letter next time I head
on River Road (sans "North")*

North Adam McCune ;)

(Author's note: I couldn't resist adding "North" to my name...)

McCune's Manchester
August 14th, 2008

Do you ever take different routes to common places you go to? I do. It always makes things more interesting. Sometimes, you're amazed at what you see and what you haven't seen. For example, take my trip up North River Road on Monday.

North River Road starts off in one of those swirling dervishes of roadways, the spaghetti junction that is the Amoskeag rotary. It takes a leap of faith to trust the sign and head North, but going under the rotary, you're greeted with a portion that is distinctly River Road. It's a thick residential section of town bordered by one of the city's many Brady Sullivan properties and followed immediately by the entry level housing of apartment complexes like Colonial Village. It's a stark contrast to the opposite side of the street, where the old colonial homes and salt box houses of Manchester's more well-to-do citizens reside.

The evidence of our wet summer is everywhere here, with thriving Hostas and other plants, near puddles of mud. Its a scene not unlike the housing.

Driving past Stark Park, there's a sign reminding you that this is one of Manchester's "walkable neighborhoods" though the nefarious news stories coming out of this very park might lead you to believe otherwise.

A giant beautiful field matches with glorious architecture of the sprawling Youth Detention Center. Such a beautiful place, with such awful stories. I feel sorry for the people who live directly across the street. I wonder if they've ever had their in-law apartment broke into by some runaway from the YDC.

Not far past the Youth Detention Center, there is a stretch of town that has always been a decent area. It's North End, yet approachable. It's near the river, but it's not pretentious. Here is where you'll find the heart and soul of the city, even if it is out of the way.

The big curve near Gingris Avenue and sweeping hill that extends beyond it warns of change to come.

Nicer homes, more landscaping, rock walls and rock gardens bring you up into the border of the city's North End, and eventually to the area's best and brightest at the Derryfield School. Literally within the stretch of one mile of road, you find a collection of kids doing community service to get out of trouble, and then an entirely different collection of kids doing community service to get into an Ivy League school. I wonder if Sara Silverman ever laughed about that during her tenure at Derryfield.

You're thrust immediately out of the residential neighborhood when you enter the bridge overpass on 93. The old viney plants frame the edge of the bridge as you pass over the muddled masses of traffic working their way to places unknown. Any time of day or night, cars pass carrying people to their destinations. Where are all these people going? What are they doing?

Then, it's Southern New Hampshire University, a good example of a good school getting better. I can almost hear the kids across the highway thumbing their nose at the idea of being a Penman. It's a shame, it's a good school and it's right here. But you can't fault a kid in any high school for playing favorites. They learn soon enough.

Some of the dorm rooms just before Webster Hall remind me of some futuristic idealized commune some hippy from the 60's could only dream of. Again, it's in contrast to the more classic architecture of Webster Hall. It's one of those "modern" buildings that suddenly turned dated when The Jetson's didn't become a reality.

The sharp turn after Webster Hall sneaks up on you, and if you're not careful you'll slide right into the trees. But a 90 degree right-hand turn takes you in towards Hooksett, a town looking more and more like Manchester "North".

In my Monday evening drive, I saw North River Road with new eyes, seeing for the 1000th time and the first time, with its obvious traits and intricacies.

Maybe it's time to take another drive.

Last Theater Heads off into Sunset

Movies have changed. We started seeing more and more 3-D movies a couple of years ago. Avatar is a classic example of this. The style of movies has even changed. Starting with The Matrix, and moving towards films like "300", we see these heavily stylized movies, almost ahead of plot and action.

So if the movies have changed, why not movie theaters?

Still, it was a sad day when the Manchester Regal Cinema 9 closed down. Nicer, newer theaters in close places like Hooksett probably forced the decision.

Now, we have Red Box and Netflix replacing a lot of our Blockbusters and other movie rental stores. Things change, business changes, but we can still mourn those changes.

McCune's Manchester
September 11th, 2008

We are about to become a movie-less city.

On September 21st the Manchester movie theater, the Regal Cinema 9 just off South Willow Street is going to shut down. It's the victim of a bad economy, poor decisions by the movie executives and probably a little bit of bad location.

With the closing of the Bedford Mall Regal location last year, that leaves Hooksett as the last bastion of movie-going for our city. And the Hooksett Regal location is no longer showing new releases. Instead, they will show movies that are a little older, called second run movies, for just $3.50. That's a far cry from the hefty $15 down the highway for the new iMax screen.

I love movies. Every now and then, I still pop in my DVD copy of "The Good, the Bad and the Ugly" and marvel at its production. It's such a different movie than the garbage that's churned out today. Sometimes you have to go out of the way to catch a flick.

Last weekend I did just that. I hopped in the car, drove up to Concord and watched the new documentary on Fear and Loathing in Las Vegas writer Hunter S. Thompson called "Gonzo" at the Red River Theatre. The movie was all right, but it was the whole of the experience that caught my attention.

It left me wondering, "Why can't Manchester have an independent movie theater?"

I have to tell you, my fiancé and I had some pretty serious discussions about doing just that a few years ago. The problem is that it's nearly impossible to make money.

Typically, the studios take 100% of the take on big movies for opening weekend. That means that when Batman was showing every penny from the ticket sales went back to the studio. Usually, that rate goes down week to week, letting the theaters themselves keep small percentages of that money. The theaters made their money on popcorn and soda.

For an independent movie, the thinking is much more

"dutch."

The independent studios split more of the ticket sales with the theaters themselves, mostly because those movies don't do as well. Those theaters, like Red River, also charge less per screening. "Gonzo" was $5, for example.

So how would it work in Manchester? Well, the Millyard is begging for something like this. Imagine a nice big ground level pad showing independent movies and documentaries at night, when parking in the Millyard is not a problem. I imagine a place that serves some decent food, maybe one that could double as a restaurant.

We need something like this. But, as a business plan, it's crazy. That's why they decided to go with a non-profit model in Concord.

Suddenly, watching a movie feels a little more like watching Public Television.

I saw "Gonzo" in the screening room, with a group of 19 year olds that acted as though they had stolen a copy of Fear and Loathing in Las Vegas -the movie, from their older brother and thought it would be cool to yell quotes at the screen. Basically, the room had a feel of an office or at least a Spartan living room with about 30 chairs arranged in successive arches away from the projection screen. This was certainly no iMax. Still, the entire time was enjoyable.

Now is the time. If there was ever an opportunity to have something like this in Manchester, it's now. There are NO movie theaters in our city's zip code. Wouldn't it be nice to have a feather in our cap like the Red River Theatre?

Think about it, with the price of oil still high, people are traveling less and less. We might even see a shift in suburbia. More people want to be closer to work and closer to home. So, having something like this close could be a real boon. It would provide a much needed shot of culture for us, and probably push for other similar businesses to come into our city. The way it stands right now, we are a three college city with no movie theater. Does that make sense?

For now, I guess I'll be stuck driving or staying in and watching my Clint Eastwood DVD's.

Surviving the Ice Storm

There was nothing I could do but write exactly what I saw the morning after the Ice Storm. We grouped together in those days afterward. It was nice to see a collective of people gathering over a common problem.

This whole column was more or less a running commentary, my collection of notes from the weekend. I kept writing down things as they happened and just put them in order. It is a bit scrambled, in the sense of good writing, but it works, mixing with that same feeling from that harsh weekend of the ice storm.

McCune's Manchester
December 16th, 2008

If the parking lots at area Dunkin Donuts are any indication, the first thing we need in an emergency is our coffee.

Imagine, 322,000 homes were not brewing their Mr. Coffees this past weekend. That's where our prized Dunkin Donuts come into play. I rely on them for my caffeine addiction. They're also responsible for New England children growing up thinking that the word "doughnuts" is really spelled D-o-n-u-t-s.

Every Dunkin's I passed Friday morning was packed. Cars full of tired, cold, angry people crammed the parking lots in search of their morning joe.

Area hardware stores reported runs on generators as soon as their doors opened. Judging by the lines at Double D's, I'm guessing most of those people generator shopping were clutching a white Styrofoam cup with their precious hot coffee with extra-extra inside.

The thought of spending the day trapped inside the house with no heat, no cable and no electricity and no where for the kids to go was unsettling. That scenario without coffee? Downright unbearable.

I passed through neighborhoods in the city where one house would have power and the next would not. I could almost see the arguments starting when one neighbor's Christmas lights would come on and the other was still stuck without a running refrigerator.

At home, we had coffee. We had power, we had heat. Only cable and Internet were out.

We occupied the kids for a while. We set up a fort in the living room, the ultimate kid's castle. We ate lunch inside. The neighbor's grandson stopped by and the kids ran around and played for a couple of hours. Then his father came over and described the situation at their home off Wallace Road in Goffstown. Snapped off trees, barely able to get out and escape to Grandma and Grandpa's, he didn't know when they would have power back.

Our cable miraculously came back sometime that afternoon. My boss at the radio station sent me an e-mail on the essentials for the weekend. We were back on the air, and trying to hold up our end of the community service bargain.

I talked to my other neighbor, Bob, whose house was on the next street over.

"No power here. I need electricity to keep the pellet stove going." He said. He ended up running an extension cord to another neighbor's generator.

He was one of the many people who installed a pellet stove this summer in preparation for the winter. It was a good idea when fuel oil was $4.00 a gallon. Now, I think he was rethinking that plan.

On Saturday, our family hit the stores to join the hoards of others doing what we as American's do in a time of crisis: Shop.

Apparently, being trapped inside after a weekend with the family, there was little left to talk about. At the Target in Bedford, I saw scores of people shopping for board games. I overheard a conversation between two customers.

"Well, we are just so bored out of our minds." A woman said, pushing a cart full of games like "Life", "Connect Four" and the notoriously lengthy game, "Monopoly".

"I know, we're at each other's throats!" Another woman said, browsing over the same games.

Our next stop was to the grocery store.

The Hannaford off Mast Road greeted customers with a sign directing them to the Bedford location if they needed frozen goods. The Goffstown store was still open, but the back half of the store was dark. The only electrical items working were a few sparse lights and the cash registers. No music, no 60 cycle hum from the freezers. It was an eerie moment. Shoppers looked at each other with weird smirks, pushing their carts in the silence.

It was an awful scene deeper in the store. Company policy and health codes prevented them from doing anything but throwing out every perishable item. The freezers were being emptied by the stock boys. One of them let out a fake cry as a coworker pushed a cart-load of partially melted ice cream to the back.

Saturday night, we did as just about everyone who had power did. We hosted relatives. My fiancé's sister, her husband and their little one came over for a hot shower and a warm meal. Making the most of the situation, we grilled burgers and chicken, pretending to have a summer picnic.

The air was thick that night. I walked out onto our deck, taking in the dangerously beautiful landscape. The layer of ice glowed off the limbs on trees, highlighted by the nearly full moon. It was striking. Moreover, it was potentially deadly. At any moment there was a sense that a limb or tree could snap. Maybe our house was next? The hum from the generators was purring in the background. Gallons of gasoline were being burned in the name of unfrozen pipes.

Monday, I was back on the air, taking calls and relaying people's harrowing stories from the weekend.

Many callers were still without power. One woman said she was home sick with the flu Friday as a giant oak tree fell and hit her trailer. Another soon fell on the other end of her home. She went down the street to her sister's house, only to have her sister back into her car when she left for work. She was not alone in the "bad weekend" department.

One of my coworkers told me he was waiting in line at Julien's Kitchen this weekend. The line was trailing outside for those waiting for a hot meal. Everyone standing, waiting, with no better place to go. He said a PSNH truck passed by. Everyone applauded. It's a moment like that, when everyone realizes the complexity and difficulty in the work they do that makes you proud to stand by your friends and neighbors.

(Author's note: How many of those generators purchased during the ice storm ended up never being used again, or even sold in the classifieds? I'm still tempted to snag one for ourselves...maybe next time, we won't be so lucky.)

Traveling Toward a Renewed Christmas Spirit

Who doesn't love a good Christmas story?

McCune's Manchester

December 24th, 2008

To us, it was a Christmas miracle. For the Marc and Jodi Abad household, it's a tradition.

Last year, we strapped the kids in the car, and drove around on Christmas Eve night, admiring the decorations on people's homes.

I think it was a last-ditch effort to force ourselves into the holiday spirit. We drove around, finding cute displays and dazzling lights. It wasn't working. We all had that sour mood that comes to some around the holidays. Endless planning, decorating, preparing for relatives that never came, and throwing a wedding in the middle of it had finally taken its toll on us. So when we were driving home, heading out on 114A, we decided to make one final detour after a group of lights caught our eye. We drove down Stephens Drive in Bedford and finally discovered that Christmas spirit.

On the street, at one household, there were wonderful displays of lights, neon reindeer, giant lighted semi-circles that were 12 feet high, a brightly lit Ferris wheel with Rudolph, Santa and Frosty as its passengers. The scene was an absolute boon for PSNH. And next door, was a single, solitary, lighted Grinch. We laughed, loosening up our own Grinchy-belts. We drove further down the street and found the real moment.

There, perched at the exact end of the cul-de-sac, was a miniature Santa's Workshop. The tiny hut was just big enough for Santa and Mrs. Claus to sit on a bench, and talk to children that come up. A rainbow colored picket fence framed either side of the workshop, and Santa greeting us, the surprise visitors that we were, with his usual jolly laugh.

For my two boys, it was absolute magic. I guess the same could be said for my wife and I. The fact that we stumbled on this scene, and Mr. and Mrs. Claus seemed almost like fate.

Every year, Marc and Jodi Abad host the elder Santa and Mrs. Claus (who bear a striking resemblance to Jodi's parents...) between Thanksgiving and Christmas for an hour every night. Children and parents come by and sit with the festive couple and talk about the gifts they hope to receive, and of course, if they've been naughty or nice this year. During such a busy time, it warms my heart to think there are people, I mean, Santa, would take the time to do something so sweet and wonderful. Their reward is the smiles they get back.

It's good know that Santa still holds some clout with the younger set. Kids today are built different than we were. Everything is so fast. Digital this, and digital that. Touch screens, Instant messages, and texts. Today's youth have lost their innocence, yet Santa gives the kids one more chance to reclaim that old innocence and be kids yet again. I think Santa is a reminder for us all to slow down.

I recall the magic that was Santa when I was a child. I also recall the whole idea coming into question when we went shopping one day and saw a Santa on every corner. My mother quickly recovered and reminded me that they were all just Santa's Helpers.

Sadly, tonight, Santa and Mrs. Claus won't be out. They found that last year's schedule, split between Santa's yearly trip and getting in some last minute guests to talk shop was too much even for Christmas magic.

Instead, they had to leave and prepare for tonight's work.
I still believe in Santa Claus, he comes and visits us every year on Stephens Drive in Bedford.

Family

Broden Gets a Lesson in Giving

Broden is a special kid. I know everyone says that about their own. I can almost hear my Scottish grandmother saying "every mama crow thinks theirs is the blackest." Which is true. But I've always known there is something about him that sets him apart.

This column was deeply personal, and I must have changed it a dozen times before I handed it in. I immediately regretted it. Did I do the right thing? Should I even mention my son like this? Talking about my family like this was a first step in something of a calling card of mine.

I had an outpouring of support after this came out, and I think that showed me that I need to be personal with what I say, or I'm never really saying anything.

Broden is still a giving child, for the most part. There are moments when he doesn't want to share his toys with this little brother, but he thinks about the food bank when we are at the grocery store. He understands where those cans and boxes go and it's largely because of the day's events I chronicled in this column.

The other theme to come out of this column was the sense that we are losing something. At the end, I talk about being self aware, and how few people really are these days. It's true, and sadly so.

**McCune's Manchester
November 27th, 2008**

Saturday was a turning point for my five year old son, Broden.

I was working, helping the Food Bank and New Horizon's collect food as part of 96.5 the Mill's Tons of Turkeys event. My son was with me to observe.

His school had been collecting cans for their food drive. Each day when I picked him up from school, he would talk about the food they collected. Usually the conversation was sprinkled with a couple of questions.

He didn't understand hunger. It didn't make sense that someone who was hungry didn't just eat.

His notion of hungry was when he's sitting on the couch on a Saturday, wanting a snack between breakfast and lunch.

So, I wanted him to see what it meant. In between looking at his Star Wars magazine and playing with the Thanksgiving decorations, he would watch as people lined up at Hannaford, bought a turkey, and gave it away. He would see first hand that not everyone gives. That's okay. Its not everyone's "thing." One person working there said it was like playing in the sandbox when you were a kid.

"Some kids would share, some would just make sure they never let go of their shovel," she said. It was so true. Today, my son would give up his shovel.

We had been at it for a while when our own hunger begged us to take a break. In the store's break room, we bought a snack and a soda. I let him keep the change, which amounted to a nickel.

His concept of money is like his concept of time. It's either day or night. With money, it's not a dollar or five cents, it's either money or none. So he slid his treasure into his pocket and we got back to work.

We were up front for a couple of minutes when I saw

him out of the corner of my eye walk up to the cash donation bin. He reached into his pocket, found his new nickel and a stray penny stuck in there and dropped it in.

I don't think I've even been more proud.

It was three years ago when he and I were in this same store and I was confronted with a dilemma. I was newly divorced, and as anyone who has gone through it knows, that puts a strain on finances. I had a cartload of groceries bagged and ready to go when the cashier told me my debit card was denied.

I knew I was cutting it close, and pay day was a week away. My son needed to get juice. Luckily I had a choice. I put the groceries on credit.

Literally, I'm still paying for that juice.

On this day, we were helping people who didn't have a Discover card. And there was my son, dropping his precious coins into the bin.

After we finished, we went down to the food bank so he could see where all of our efforts were going. The tireless Executive Director, Melanie Gosselin and some of the other workers showed us around. My son saw where the cans go that he picks out when we do our shopping. It's his job to pick out one item and put it in every time we go.

He watched as a forklift unloaded a pallet of freshly delivered turkeys, part of more than 39 tons of food donated on that one day.

These are trying times, and it was a day like Saturday that helps me remember our potential. It's our potential as a city, state and country to stand together and help. It's not a political idea, it knows no party affiliation. It only knows the end result is good.

After we were done, I took my boy to Wal-Mart where he picked out a toy. It was "Echo-Echo from Ben 10 Alien Force." Whatever it was, it was special. And he deserved it.

I hope everyone reading this has a great Thanksgiving. I know what I'm thankful for. I'm thankful that I have a son that is beginning to understand the world around him. In today's world, a person who is self-aware is unfortunately a rarity. But that's just my two cents.

Or maybe my son's six cents.

It Was No Time For a Snowstorm

What in the hell were we thinking? A December wedding...in New Hampshire?

We had actually planned on a summer wedding, but when that fell through, we decided to kill two birds with one stone. We would have a wedding near Christmas, that way, my parents could come out, stick around for the holiday with the boys and go back home.

Mother Nature had a different plan. Their flight was cancelled and they missed the wedding all together.

Still, we had a great time. It was perfect, especially for us.

The Strange Brew might be a strange place for someone to have a reception. For us, it was awesome. It capped off a night that was fun, exciting and embodied my new family.

The best part of the evening was the limo ride.

Normally, it's a quiet time for newlyweds to share

between the ceremony and the reception. For us, we strapped our two boys into car seats with us and cranked up the radio, all of us singing along to Bob Seger's "Travelin' Man" in the back. That moment, that picture of us, is etched in my brain forever. I cherish it.

McCune's Manchester
December 26th, 2008

That first snow storm of the season is usually the worst. In our most recent case, it came at the worst time.

I began shoveling at 6:00am Saturday. Under normal circumstances, I wouldn't have ventured out that early on a weekend to shovel. But this Saturday was different. You see, Saturday was my wedding day.

I didn't know how many people were going to make the trip to Hudson for the ceremony itself, but I was sure the number of people would be a little larger when we came closer to home for the reception at the Strange Brew. The place is special to us.

It was a few years ago, on a much warmer summer day when we agreed to meet, being setup by a mutual friend. We were supposed to wait for each other out front. I sat there outside, clammy hands, nervously pacing in my new clothes. I wanted to make a good impression. I waited for what seemed like forever when I realized I had been stood up.

I went inside, ready to have a cold one. Then I saw her. She was scanning the bar for me, probably in the same state of disbelief when I came up to her and said "hi."

We sat across from each other. I was hoping she

couldn't feel my nervous anticipation. I tried to catch her eyes as we sat and enjoyed each other's company and the beer selection. I remember distinctly. She had a Newcastle, and I had a Sierra Nevada Porter.

In the middle of our first date, we had an intruder. There was this guy, who introduced himself as a chef at a local restaurant, and he kept trying to butt in on our conversation. It wasn't until about a half hour in that I realized he was trying to pick up my date.

A little of my Alpha-male appeared that night. Instead of lions fighting each other on the plains of Africa, I fought him off with the only weapon I had. Words.

We've laughed at that moment since then. He unwittingly brought us closer with his cheesy pick-up.

In the years since we've come back to the Strange Brew on dates. Its had a special place in our hearts. We've been there on packed nights, and quiet evenings. We've danced to the blues band, we've bellied up to the bar. And more importantly, I think I've tried every beer on that lengthy menu.

So when we were planning the wedding, it was the first place that came to mind when we started talking about the reception. We didn't know how they would receive the idea, and we weren't even sure if they would do it. But Mitch and Dee were more than accommodating. Basically, they opened four hours early so we could squeeze in the reception before normal hours. It was perfect.

I've wondered what would have happened had I just given up that summer night a few years ago. Both of us had our share of relationship mishaps in the years before and I'm sure we both would have seen this as a sign to steer clear. I'll chalk that one up to my thirst for a good beer as the reason we made it.

Back to Saturday, I finished shoveling. My five year old was up now and we got ready together. I wasn't supposed to be at home that morning. I was supposed to be at my parent's hotel. When I got up on Friday, we found out the bad news; their flight had been canceled.

To make it worse, no amount of bargaining, pleading or haggling with the airline did any good. The earliest they could arrive would be 11:30pm, the night of our wedding. So they canceled the whole trip. It was a bummer.

Not that it hasn't happened before. When my parents were married, they decided on a winter wedding as well, January 15th. But my Grandmother, my mother's mother couldn't make it. It was 20 below zero that day in Wisconsin, and my Grandmother had spent years in quarantine with Tuberculosis. Her limited lung function literally took her breath away on days like that. So perhaps it's a family tradition.

My thoughts drifted around this as my son and I loaded up in the car and set out. The roads were awful.

People forget in about six months time what it's like to drive in hazardous conditions. I had the radio on, and the voice was crackling out "stay off the roads unless absolutely necessary today." I believe I fit under that qualification.

When we finally arrived at the chapel, I was blown away. The room was packed. Only a few chairs up front were open, and those were going to remain that way because of my parent's absence.

We had taken the time to put the car seats in the back

of the limo, so my five year old and our soon-to-be two year old could ride along with us. It couldn't have been any more fitting. The four of us, sliding off on the slippery roads, ready to start our lives together.

He Came Close to Losing his Home, but not his Pride

Looking back, this is a sign of things to come.

Our house lost over $50,000 of value in a couple of years time. We were not alone. Many houses lost value, and homes started to go into foreclosure. We were slowly inching closer to becoming a sad statistic.

They got it wrong. We should have never bailed out the people responsible. If anything, part of the thread of American ingenuity is failure, because through it, comes innovation and business savvy. Let them fail, and watch when someone swoops in to restore order. That's business, and that was the right tact to take. Instead, we've gotten deeper into a mess that is more tangled by the day.

McCune's Manchester
October 2nd, 2008

With the Federal bank bailout, the issue of "Main Street vs. Wall Street" couldn't hit harder than it does on my street.

We've had a few foreclosures on our dead-end Pinardville road. We've had a number of houses, including ours, that have been up for sale. Some of them, like ours, never sold.

Typically, what happened in our home would be private. But I think it's important to tell you about it, considering all of the financial talk buzzing around.

Here's our scenario.

We have two kids. When my youngest son was born, we knew it was time to move. Our quaint, two bedroom, 800 square foot house was too cramped for four people. The market had yet to tank, so we listed it. And waited. We dreamed of a four bedroom cape with an office overlooking a nice yard where the kids would play.

We watched in disbelief as the bottom of the market fell apart. No one came to look at our tiny house. We soon realized we were stuck. But we needed action because of our loan.

We had an ARM loan, an Adjustable Rate Mortgage, that was going to go up to an unbearable 8% followed by a loan-shark-rate of 10% the following year. In essence, we were some of those people you've heard about. The loan was very clearly intended to be refinanced, but with the tightening of purse strings, that became nearly impossible.

We went to the bank for help. They told us that most lenders were now using the rule that if your house had been on the market in the last year, you could not refinance.

What? We were now in a panicked state. For a couple of months, we thought we were going to be a statistic. One of those masses that gets foreclosed on. Worry blankets all of your decisions when you go through something like this, and I don't envy anyone that has.

Our last hope was FHA. They would refinance, as long as we passed our inspection. They needed to inspect the home, and with our wet winter last year, our crawlspace was a little damp.

I spent a weekend in the basement, slouched over, pounding the concrete with a jack hammer to clear out a new drain to our sump pump. My back was nearly destroyed in the process, but in the end I did what every man could only hope to do in that situation. I saved our house.

We got refinanced.

Our victory was short-lived. We still had a problem of space. Now our son was getting older. We desperately needed more room. Our next goal was to add-on.

Not so fast, slick.

With the drop in home prices, we couldn't. Our new assessed value wouldn't allow for us to get a loan to finance a meager one-room addition. As it stands today, our answer for more space has been temporarily bandaged with a shed to house some household items. For the time being, our youngest will still have to sleep in his crib in our room.

You can throw around buzz words like "Predatory lending" or "Foreclosure" but when the dust settles, it's people like me who will be on the outside looking in. We found ourselves in a financial mess. We found a solution to get out of it. No bailouts, no handouts from anyone. And what will be our reward? Nothing. Instead, people on either side of our situation will be rewarded.

I wonder how many other people out there are part of this gray statistic. How many more people saw the trouble coming and were able to get out of the way?

I've counted my blessing that we still have a place to stay. We beat the odds and came out on top. That's the story on our street.

Thanks to Goldenrod, Ice Cream in Favor

How can anyone, especially my son, who was born in Wisconsin... the DAIRY STATE, not like ice cream? It has boggled my mind since he was a baby. He never liked it, until Goldenrod. After we went there on this particular trip, he started to enjoy ice cream.

To this day, he still doesn't like milk. He eats cheese, loves yogurt, but won't touch a big glass of cold milk for anything. It still amazes me.

I had fun writing this column, bringing the past and present together with sports. It felt natural to talk about all of these things in context to something as eternal and important as ice cream.

McCune's Manchester
June 26th, 2008

My five year old son has never been a big fan of ice cream.

Seriously, he's never cared for it. No ice cream and no frosting. I wonder if there is a test he can take at the Elliot to see if he's okay.

Actually, that's not necessary anymore because we finally brought him to a Manchester staple: Goldenrod.

Candia Road is newly paved in front of the

Goldenrod, but not much else has changed since it opened 57 years ago.

It was Saturday, glorious weather when we made a surprise stop.

"Where are we?" My son inquired from the back seat.

"We've just got to make a quick stop. Don't worry, it's a fun place." I told him.

Our real purpose was to grab a gift certificate for my fiancé's father. He's been going there since he learned to ride a bike. That was when the New York Giants were still the "local" team and the Red Sox were still breaking hearts. He used to bike to the Goldenrod and back home, ice cream cone in hand, in time for the kickoff for the Giants games on Sundays.

My son is growing up in a very different world. The New York Giants are now the enemy, and he's been spoiled by the run of Red Sox championships recently.

When the world around us is changing so rapidly, it's nice to ground ourselves at a place that hasn't changed a bit. That ground is certainly the Goldenrod.

"Do you want anything?" I asked my son.

"Just a lemonade." He replied, sounding a little unsure.

I ordered a neutral flavor that I thought he might like...Graham Cracker and we sat down. He sipped his lemonade in the hot sun, eying my cup of tan frozen cream.

"Do you want some?" I asked, knowingly emulating the same expression my mother might have given 25 years ago in a similar circumstance.

"Okay." He said, with an unsure frown.

"You don't have to, I just think you might like it." I replied in my most friendly tone, grinning like the

Cheshire cat.

"No, I want to." Was he trying it just to please me?

I scraped a little ice cream on the end of my plastic spoon and held it up, waiting for him to respond. I wanted to see the reaction of the-boy-who-doesn't-like-ice-cream.

His eyes lit up. "Mmmmmmm, that's good!" he said. We split the rest of the ice cream and traded our thoughts on how good it tasted.

The Giants are the enemy, the Red Sox are champions, and my five year old now loves his ice cream. I guess some things are meant to change.

He's a Sucker for Lola, Despite her Missing Hair

My wife has more than occasionally pointed out that it was my idea to get Lola, not hers. I still say we have her because my wife loves animals so much. But I'm the one who suggested a Bulldog.

To be frank, there are times that I've really questioned that wisdom. She's a pain in the butt. She's stubborn, and after years of abuse, she was not entirely housebroken when we got her. There are moments when she cowers and runs to the corner, usually when we are getting pans out of the cupboard. Either the noise, or the large, metal object startle her. It makes me think that years ago someone hit her with something, perhaps a shovel. I get angry just thinking about it.

I can happily say that Lola has all her hair now, and eventually her personality has started to come through. At first, she had no idea what to make of us. Now, she's happy to see us. She begs for food, and even sits in anticipation while we get hers ready.

She's staring at me while I'm typing this right now. It's almost like she knows I'm writing about her.

Animals are such a big part of our family. Growing up, we had dogs, cats, chickens, turkeys and even pigs, so I'm used to their presence. Having them around feels normal, nurturing and like home.

Lola has wormed her way into our hearts.

McCune's Manchester
November 5th, 2009

I don't know what we were thinking.

Well, actually, I do. But it still was a decision that I chalk up to my wife's big heart.

We adopted a dog. It wasn't like we needed another dog. We have a perfectly fine dog; a giant mutt named Wilbur that sleeps 23.95 hours of the day on our bed.

For months, my wife has been saying she wanted another dog. We had a second dog, a Boston Terrier named Rocky. He died just before my youngest son was born.

We were coming up on three years of a one-dog household, so I guess it was time for our peace to be disturbed.

We made a deal. We would look. If we saw a sweet Boston Terrier, we would almost be obliged to adopt him or her. But if we saw an English Bulldog, we would have to consider. I threw that curve-ball in, I've always been partial to Bulldogs, and it ended up slapping me in the face.

It all started with a nice family weekend away in
Maine. We were going to enjoy the autumn air near Old
Orchard Beach and relax. First, we had to visit a local vet
that doubled as an animal shelter.

For my wife, it's important to her that we adopt a dog.
There are a lot of options out there, but that was a
prerequisite. My wife has a big heart, it's one of her best
qualities, and for her, the bigger the sob story for an
animal, the more she falls in love.

There she was. Lola, an English Bulldog so sweet and
loving, she came over and plopped down right on my
lap. She had been neglected. She was missing hair, her
ears were a mess, and our vet said she had a bacterial
skin infection. Bulldogs require constant maintenance;
you have to clean their ears and their silly folds of skin
around their face and their tail.

We drove home with Lola facing the wrong way in the
back seat, a two hour drive, with a rear-facing dog.

She has a face only a mother could love, and her tail
looked like some mess she might leave in the back yard.
It was mostly bald, with a tuft of hair poking out the top.
Her skin was bright pink underneath her white and
brown hair. So many problems...so of course, my wife
fell in love.

I say it was my wife's idea, but I tell you, that stupid
dog has wormed her way into my heart as well. She's
sweet and loving, and runs around in a crazed circle
when I come home from work.

She has a defiant streak. When we scolded her for
trying to go on the couch, directing her to her bed, she
walked straight over and peed on her bed while looking
right at us. She's just as stubborn as everyone else in this

household.

So many things can go wrong with a new pet. What if she doesn't get along with our other dog? What if the kids don't like her? What if she doesn't like the kids? What if she snaps and starts tearing up the furniture?

So far, so good. She's already a part of this family and it looks like she's here to stay. Our new, stinky, partially hairless, ugly-as-sin dog has joined our family. The worst part is that she is that she fits right in.

Time Apart Puts it Together

I think my wife is afraid of the mental image I paint of her in my column. She silently worries about what people think about her based on only what I say.

Even this column, I mention when I wake her up that she is "much different than..Sleeping Beauty" Well that isn't fair, really. Who is nice when they wake up from a dead sleep?

For the record, my wife is the kindest, gentlest person I've ever met. She's smart, beautiful, funny, sweet and she's mine. So, whatever mental image you have of my better half, I hope you keep that in mind. That is what I truly think about her.

McCune's Manchester
December 17th, 2009

This past weekend, my wife went away to New York City, spending some much needed time with her friend Christine. They went to the Guggenheim, watched the skaters at Rockefeller Center, shopped at the downtown Macy's, and ate their way around the city.

Back at home, I spent the weekend with the boys, spending my time wiping boogery noses, watching drivers skate by us on 293, shopping at the downtown Wal-Mart, and eating our way around the city.

I guess I had forgotten how much I appreciate my wife. This coming weekend, my wife and I will celebrate our first wedding anniversary. It has been quite a year. If you've followed this column through 2009, you know exactly what I mean. Through it, my partner and I have remained strong, hopefully building the foundation for our years to come.

Perhaps the fairy-tale romance you hear about when you are younger doesn't exist. I'm certainly no Prince Charming, and if you wake my wife from a dead sleep, her reaction is much different than that of Sleeping Beauty. But a real, lasting marriage isn't built on Disney movie plots. Sometimes, it is cemented in good-old-fashioned hardship.

When I was with my sons this weekend, I remembered how much I used to do as a single parent. The usual chore of cleaning the house becomes a respite from the constant noise of children. Getting dressed and loading everyone into a car to go somewhere isn't just a task, it's a triumph of wills. I went to a holiday party at a friends house on Saturday night, forgetting there would be no other parent to run the normal "interference", so that I could actually have an adult conversation and maybe have some food beyond the half-a-cookie my youngest son discarded in favor of something else.

I'm not complaining, I enjoy every minute with my

boys, I'm just drawing your attention to the amount of work it takes to care for children. You could equate it to how people talk about exercise. They complain about working out, telling their friends how hard it is, but still see enjoyment in it. So raising children is like exercise, only the end result is much different; parents tend to get fatter.

I hate to admit that it took a weekend alone with my children to truly appreciate my better half again. This relationship attrition can be healthy. After all, they say that distance makes the heart grow fonder. Perhaps that is still true if that distance just means a moment of peace and quiet during a hectic weekend.

When my wife and I were wed a year ago, we nearly had to say our vows in a large snow-bank. Our countless hours of planning our nuptials, and planning the right date to match everyone's schedules resulted in us picking December 20th for our wedding date. It was the first of many lessons you learn as a couple, and that lesson is not to plan your life around everyone else. Instead, you have to do what is right by each other.

So, in the traditional sense, your first anniversary wedding gift is supposed to be something made of paper. I guess that makes my column this week my gift to her. She's reading this right now in her pajamas at our kitchen table, between sips of coffee and carefully cutting bagels and preparing oatmeal for the boys. She has no idea I wrote this for her. I wish you could see the look on her face right now.

Hildegaard is Dying But a Piece of her Will Live

On

Oh, sweet Hildegaard. Her passing was a tough one. I won't say I cried, but I was close to it. It was because I gave up the dream, or so I thought. Replacing her with another similar car was the right move.

It is kind of silly how much these old cars have worked their way into my own personality.

That car represented my own rebirth. I became my own person again after I bought her, and fixing her gave me a sense of pride, knowing I had accomplished something on my own.

My father used to make fun of me for not being able to work on cars. At one point, he had been a mechanic, and I think he saw my lack of concern about car maintenance as a character flaw. He used to jokingly call me "Mr. Goodwrench."

It wasn't without trying. My first car was a 1972 Volkswagen Super Beetle. I thought I was a king in that thing. It had all sorts of problems, all of them were beyond my mechanical know-how.

So, Hildegaard was the start of something for me. I will always love that car and a piece of her will live on in every car I own in the future.

McCune's Manchester
March 4th, 2010

I love my car. To most, she's an eyesore. To me, she's a classic.

When I finally drove my 1983 Mercedes Benz Diesel wagon home a year and a half ago, it was a culmination. So many things had changed in my life, and I felt the weight of those changes lift when I drove the car.

You see, Hildegaard (yes, I named my car), is more than a vehicle to me. Around the time I bought her, I had just gone through a divorce. It wasn't easy, as that scenario in life never is for anyone. I had a car that my ex-wife and I shared, and to be honest, it didn't suit me. In fact, I hated that car. It needed to go.

When my father stumbled on this old Mercedes, I thought it was perfect. The engine had been overhauled, it was perhaps a little beat up, but everything was working in spite of all it had been through. I could relate. My father drove to inspect it, bought it with my blessing and parked it at my parent's house in Wisconsin.

It took a couple years for it to make it to New Hampshire. In that time, I would visit it while my new family grew and we traveled to visit my parents. We would drive her around, as I hoped for the day that I could finally bring her home.

That was last August. I poured over that car, scrubbing, cleaning, changing bulbs, and making sure she was up to snuff for the state inspection.

It was then that I found it. On the floor of the back seat, some oil had spilled, and I had to tear up the carpets to clean it up. It was nasty, grimy stuff, the kind that had been sitting for years, and it took the better part of the afternoon to finally get rid of it. Peeling back the carpets, I felt something move. It was small and metal, about the size of a quarter. I grabbed it and rushed into the house to clean off the old oil and was amazed at what I saw.

The water and soap turned dark brown as it washed away, revealing the words "Republica Italiana." I was shocked. It was a 100 Lire coin; Italian currency. But how did it get in my car?

Turn back the clock to 1982, when my car was a brand-new model. The dollar was enjoying a robust surge against foreign currency, and savvy car dealers seized on an opportunity. They would travel to Europe, buy fleets of new, European cars, ship them to America, and sell them state-side, undercutting companies like Mercedes. Car manufacturers hated these guys, called "gray-market" dealers. Honestly, they were just smart American businessmen, enjoying the fruits of our old-fashioned national ingenuity as well as the vulnerability of foreign fiat currencies.

My coin, most likely slipped out of some Italian dealer's pocket and wedged itself in between the carpets. It would travel from Italy with the car to California, where it was sold to its first owner. The years would drift by, and several new owners would drive Hildegaard until she finally found her way to me.

I bought a coin holder at Bob's Coins of Manchester on the city's West Side. The coin dangles from my rear-view mirror as a reminder of where I've been and where I'm going.

Sadly, Hildegaard is dying a slow death. This winter was hard on the old girl. Rust, a heater core, transmission problems, and now brakes are all becoming issues, forcing me to give her up. She's made it 294,000 miles and I hate to be the one to have to give up on her.

Still, a piece of her will live on. Whatever car I drive, I will take that coin and drape in on the mirror. It gives me peace, and keeps me humble as I remember that not everything is perfect. And that's okay.

These Were Days of Wine and Whiplash

Just leaving the house alone is a monumental task when you have small children. I never like feeling like a burden to anyone. It's a trait I stock up to my Scandinavian heritage. That feeling of being a burden and not wanting others to help. Putting someone else out is the worst form of guilt.

But when my wife and I get out by ourselves, there are moments when we are completely different. We get professionally silly every year at the Winter Wine Spectacular. Were it not for my wife, I would have never went to one of these events.

Now that I have, I feel like I've grown because of it.

The event is a night of 1000 networking possibilities. The food, the wine, and the cause are all so great that I can't think of a single better culmination of the those things.

In our attempt to be responsible on this particular night, we ended up getting into an accident. It was that slight twist of irony that had us laughing at the event.

And the headache? I still blame that on the accident...not the wine.

McCune's Manchester
February 4th, 2010

We were headed out.

When you become a parent, heading for a night out with your significant other is no small task. Coordinating a babysitter, a ride, and hoping that you made it out of the house without any kid paraphernalia become of paramount importance.

But we made it. Of course, I felt like a child myself. My father-in-law was driving us to our date. I recalled those days before I had my driver's license and a parent would have to drive so I could accompany a fair lady on a date. Back then, it was all anticipation. My palms would sweat, my voice would crack, I was nearly shaking because I talked a girl into coming with me. The weirdest thing? I couldn't wait to do it again.

But on this night, my wife and I were anticipating the Winter Wine Spectacular, put on by Easter Seals at the Radisson in Manchester.

After a fresh blanket of snow, we were gliding (and I do mean gliding) down the hill on Varney Street, my father-in-law, Bob, hit the brakes, avoiding the car in front of him on the suddenly slick streets. He stopped just in time, and for a moment, we just sat there in peace. Then...WHAM! Our heads whipped forward and back, as a car hit us from behind. It wasn't a hard hit. It wasn't a major accident, but just enough to give us whip lash the next day.

"So sorry, so sorry," the man in the car that rear-ended us said as he got out. We did the typical exchange of information hand off, and headed on our way again.

This was serious. We had planned on being just early enough to grab a glass, and head in as the doors were opening. Now we were late. We'd missed the start by nearly 30 minutes. We have precious few dates as a married couple with kids, and our business was to try wine. Lots of wine. And now we were late? Serious indeed.

We rushed past all the people we knew. Mike and

Tracy are here from WZID? Cool. That's great. We'll catch up with them in a minute... right now, I'd like to sample about 19 Pinot Noirs before my neck starts to hurt.

And sample we did. The wine, the food, it was all great. Easter Seals says they have 1,400 wines to sample. No, we didn't try them all. We were selective. by the time the doors close at 9:00, we are lucky to have made it around the entire room.

In fact, one of the best parts about the event is the networking opportunity it provides. I caught up with dozens of people I hadn't seen in months, including Mike and Tracy. The event offers a nice blend of professionals and connoisseurs. For my money, I've always been more likely to pick up a beer than a wine, so the event also offers a chance to try something I normally wouldn't.

I smile, and nod, sniffing the glass like I know what I'm talking about. Meanwhile, my pourer is going on and on about how this wine came from this valley, and how it is superior to all other wines of its class. For me, I'm more apt to shrug my shoulders and say "tastes pretty good to me!" and move on.

By the end of the evening, we had enough. The next day, we both woke up a little sore and a little ringing in our ears. I maintain it was from the accident.

The Unemployment Chronicles

A New Place to Hang His Work Coffee Cup

When I wrote this column, I was still in denial. It's a powerful emotion, and its pull shouldn't be overlooked.

A month into being unemployed, I started to get really scared. But when I wrote this column, I had just picked my son up from school after being let go. The gravity of what had happened hadn't sunk in yet. I think that gave this column clarity.

The part I didn't tell: The weekend before I was let go, my wife and I were taking a truncated honeymoon in Maine. We were married in December, and at the time, we couldn't afford the time or money to take a "real" honeymoon, so we promised each other this weekend away.

We had such a wonderful time. That weekend was supposed to be the start, our beginning, but soon it was the end of something else.

At one point during the weekend, we ventured out to go for a drive around Portland, Maine. There was something about that drive that was unsettling. So many establishments were out of business. It was scary and impossible not to notice. We drove by a Goodwill, and thought 'why not'?

I found the coffee mug inside that would be an ironic backdrop to being laid off. That's the coffee mug on the cover of the book, and I've since learned that you can buy them at The Christmas Tree Shop for $1.

The morning I was let go, I saw the writing on the wall. I feel like I handled the situation like a pro. By 7:00am, I called my wife and told her I was afraid I was going to lose my job. She reassured me that everything was fine and I was being silly. I still knew.

But, the show must go on. I did my final morning show the same way I had on any other day. In radio, getting fired is a part of the business. I had often fantasized about what I would say or what I would do when and if that time came. Perhaps I would say something about it on the air, or do something over-the-top.

Nope. In the end, the best thing I could do, for me, for the listener, and for the station, was to give my full attention to my final shift.

When the General Manager, Ray Garon, finally delivered the news, I could only say one word. I simply said "fuck", almost involuntarily. It wasn't in anger, it wasn't being bitter, it was just my assurance that my fears were coming true.

I can look back on those months, and that moment, and know that I've become a better person because of what happened. I'm happier now, and I love the path that this forced decision guided me on.

I had been writing for two years when I was laid off from my full time job, but I became a writer the moment I walked out those doors with that Dream Boat coffee mug in my hand.

McCune's Manchester
February 4th, 2009

My wife and I drove by a Goodwill store. I can't help it, I'm a thrifty person. That may come in handy these days. More on that in a bit.

There was something that drove me to it. It was a

white coffee mug with the words "Dream Boat" in big black letters on the side. Hilarious. For a dollar, it was worth it.

I was looking for a new coffee cup for work. It was big enough to fit two of those Green Mountain "K cups" that are all the rage.

I laughed with coworkers as I brought it in on Monday. I didn't know at the time, but it would be my last work purchase.

Monday started out like any other at the radio station. It was the day after the Super Bowl, and I was preparing to talk about the normal things. What commercials were funny, what about that catch. etc., etc.

Then one of my coworkers told me that my boss had been let go on Friday. Immediately, flags went up. If he was fired Friday, how am I just now hearing about it? I nervously prepared the rest of my show, knowing full well it might be my last.

9:00 am rolled around. One of the managers came by and said "we need to talk." My knees buckled a little as I made the frog march to the Business Managers office. Those meetings never end well in his office.

They told me it's over.

This May, it was going to be five years with the company. Most of that time as the morning host of the Mill. I was shocked.

It wasn't me, they told me. It was the economy. That's the new let-down. It's the business equivalent of "It's not you, it's me" in a relationship. It was true, as evidenced by what is on the air instead of me this morning. I was downsized. I'm a victim of the economy.

Maybe that's not the right way to really describe it.

Maybe I was mugged by the economy, stabbed in the gullet and left to bleed to death in the ditch on Wall Street.

Let me tell you, I hold no ill-will towards my former employer. Where my angst is directed is the idiotic rules and regulations like Sarbanes-Oxley that have crippled many industries, included publicly held media.

The over compensation of the problems that surfaced from the Enron scandal resulted in this hypertension version of regulation. Everything had to be checked and double checked. On its surface, that may not seem like a bad thing. But dig a little deeper and the problem shows its wicked face.

I have been in radio for ten years, as far removed from accounting as you can possibly be. Still, because of the new rules, my job was classified more for its accounting purpose than its on-air purpose.

You see, when someone is on the radio, one of the jobs they have is to dutifully mark which commercial has played. We get a paper log, and these days, it's mimicked on a computer that's playing most on-air elements. My checking off of each commercial became so scrutinized, that I became, for all intents and purposes, a part of the accounting department. In the eyes of the shareholders, that was all I was.

It was a shame really. I've done bits, interviews, crazy stunts, witty retorts, one liners, zingers, stagers, sweepers, promos and commercials. But my most important duty of the day was making sure that Spot "X" played at Time "Z". Did I mention that this was all recorded into a computer file anyway? Maybe that's what makes me so replaceable.

I'm not telling you this to sound bitter. I'm not. I am looking for a day job, that keeps me busy enough. Like I said, there is no ill-will towards anyone at my old place of employment. They did all they could. I was just another casualty of our web of failed financial policies in this country.

When my meeting was over, I shook everyone's hand, trying to hold my head high. I grabbed my packet of information about rolling over my 401k and signing up for the horribly expensive C.O.B.R.A. Insurance plan. I stacked it all neatly in a pile, and topped it off with my "Dream Boat" mug and solemnly took my last elevator ride down to my car.

That damned mug felt like a scarlet letter.

Why would anyone need their work coffee mug? Unless. Oh, yes. He must have lost his job. Poor sap.

For so long, that job has been a part of my identity, a part of who I am. My coworkers were one part friend and one part family. Now, I'll be like the rest who have been let go before their time, a leper left to fend for himself amongst a colony of his own.

Now I have to figure out where I'm going to hang my mug.

Back on the Air...but Still Looking

Slowly, I started to find my way while I was unemployed. I was secretly hoping that my plight, and talking about my situation, would result in someone reading my column and realizing they just had to have me work for their company.

At this point in the unemployment game, it was about the little victories, and the fact that my old employer still wanted me to work for them spoke volumes about me, if only to my next potential employer.

When I finally did find full-time work, I resigned from my on-air duties. In an odd twist, my two week notice and was greeted with congratulations instead of shock. That was a great moment.

At the same time, the true problems with unemployment were starting to become clear to me.

Working part time doesn't give you more money while you collect unemployment. Instead, unemployment takes that money out of your weekly check. The end result is the same money, but less time to look for a full time job and to spend with your family.

I suppose this is set up to stop abuse, but the end result is more people on unemployment choose not to join the workforce, in any form, until they get a full time job. It simply isn't worth it to work part-time.

McCune's Manchester
April 2nd, 2009

I'm back on the radio.

The last few Sunday mornings I've been back on WZID, holding down the fort.. It's not full time work, just one day a week, five and a half hours at a time. It's going to pay little more than the cable bill at this point, but it's something.

Five years ago, I rolled into town at midnight on a cool May evening in my beat up Saturn station wagon. I moved half-way across the country for an opportunity.

The job was doing Afternoons on WZID, a station that was so widely known that my old boss recognized it when I handed in my resignation back in Wisconsin.

In that time, I had survived a few other budget cuts and personnel moves. I'd endured a divorce, celebrated the birth of my second son, and a new marriage. I also took another new opportunity when I accepted my last position as morning host on 96.5 the Mill. As I've written in this space before, I was let go in February because of a budget cut that I didn't survive.

In the span since then, I've poured every ounce of energy into finding a new job. When the stories come out about long lines of people lining up for job interviews at Canobie Lake Park, you know it's bleak in the job market. It wasn't long ago that many amusement parks had to ship in Russian teenagers to fill positions. Now people with college degrees are fighting for jobs keeping the peace on the Crazy Cups.

I've come full circle in some ways. I've been amongst the people fighting for elbow room in today's economy.

In a few weeks, I'll be collecting unemployment. I can see flaws in the system already, and I'm trying to figure it out. Basically, I'll collect the maximum $425 benefit. Doing some crude math, that pays me about $10 an hour to look for a job. That also excludes me from taking a job for less than $10 an hour. Considering I would have to pay for day care for two boys to take a job, it's more like $12 an hour.

What's the incentive? At some point, this runs out. I suppose a $10 an hour job would sound fine at that point. But seriously, what incentive do the 8% of people reading this who are unemployed have to get out of the house to work?

I guess a benefits package would be worth it. Right now, our household is covered by four separate insurance plans. I'm insured through C.O.B.R.A, my five year old is insured through his mother, my other son is insured through New Hampshire Healthy Kids and my wife is insured through her work.

Trying to combine these plans into one solid plan for our household, I've applied for jobs that I never thought I would ever consider. I applied for a manager's position at a local Dunkin Donuts. Two weeks later, I received an e-mail telling me they decided to go another direction. Never have I been so depressed.

I'm not sure the best use of my abilities would be fully realized managing a Dunkin Donuts. I don't mean that as anything against anyone who does that for a living. I'm sure there are people that are fantastic at doing that job. I guess they felt I wasn't one of them.

But how many managers at Dunkin Donuts or bank tellers or stock clerks are working those jobs simply for their health insurance plan? I'm not sure if any study exists for that statistic, but my guess is that's it a large percentage. What a waste. And for what? Another insurance plan that keeps getting pared off every year by companies. My old insurance plan didn't even cover certain cancer medications because they were considered "special." I doubt my grandmother, who died of cancer, would have agree that it was so rare and unique to call any aspect of it "special."

For now, I'll continue to work my one-day-a-week job while looking for another. Knowing I'm not alone in my hunt is of little comfort. I can only hope that where headed to the bottom of this mess and we'll see the light at the end of the tunnel soon.

Tuesday was a Special Day

I selected this column because, together with the next selection, it illustrates how up-and-down your emotions are when you are unemployed. This day, Saint Patrick's day ,was a happy day. I felt I had done something good by looking for a job.

I got up, got ready, put on my suit and hit the streets, hoping to get in front of somebody that could offer me something. I was ready for anything.

Nothing happened.

Still, it was good for me, if only to cleanse my self-doubt that I wasn't doing enough. Of course, having a big Guinness to close the night doesn't hurt.

McCune's Manchester
March 19th, 2009

Tuesday night, Saint Patrick's Day's evening, was one of those nights in Manchester. It had the feeling of Primary season.

People were flooding the streets all day, but instead of chasing politicians, they were mostly just chasing green beer.

Let me get one thing straight: I hate green beer. Sacrilege? Maybe. A glance at my last name tells you enough about my Irish heritage. No where in the folklore of any old Irish tale that I know of dictates that I need to drink green beer. Or even eat cabbage for that matter.

But Tuesday was special. I started the day fighting the crowds, pounding the pavement of our fair city still looking for a job. Soon, I would trade my stuffy suit for a nice soft hooded sweatshirt and trade my list of places to drop off resumes for a list of the beers on tap at the Strange Brew. Basically, I was going to join the crowd I had cursed during the early part of the day.

I started at my usual Tuesday night stop, the Strange Brew. I found the place so packed that there was a long line waiting to get in. Earlier in the night, there had been a couple of national bands doing an acoustic set before heading over to the Verizon to open for Motley Crue.

The crowd was just starting to shuffle in to the Verizon when I began my trip downtown.

Great, more crowds to fight, I thought.

I soon joined up with my friends at the Brew, and before long we were crowded out by an unusually large crowd for a Tuesday night, even by their standards.

After a while, I finished up before getting a call from a friend of mine over at J.W. Hills. This friend is very proud of his Irish heritage. So proud in fact, that his normal rule of teetotalism is lifted for this one night out of the year. I felt a duty and a purpose to join him, if only for the Isle of Eire's sake.

At this point of the evening I stopped being a participant and started being an observer. Something was happening all around me it seemed. One moment a dance competition was starting from the stage, the next, a fight was erupting on the street. Still, for the most part, the mood was jovial. Any of those events seemed possible during the Primary season and they were happening on Saint Patty's Day.

It was a sea of green. A Dr. Seuss hat with green and white stripes, an accessory unacceptable 364 other nights of the year was the norm. On the surface, it seemed that people were missing the real meaning of the holiday. But perhaps the revelers were taking the legend of Saint Patrick driving the snakes out of Ireland by driving the snakes from themselves for the evening.

The smiles on the faces of most of the people were most likely helped by the copious amounts of alcohol consumed, but it was no matter. We were all one in the evening, a giant smiling brigade of people just enjoying a mid-week holiday. So what if they put food coloring in our beer? It was kind of fun.

The police had their hands full at times. I never have envied their jobs on nights like that. First there was the security detail of a concert, followed by the security nightmare of a downtown full of imbibers, then it was the traffic mess of the concert followed by the traffic mess of imbibers. Still, other than a few fights, it seemed the worst of the night was a rash of underage drinkers. Like I said, the police had their hands full, but they handled it well.

I left the scene and my friends as the last of the crowd from the concert was hitting the street. More smiles on the faces of the people coming out of the Verizon as they met the pavement, trying to decide if they should go home or go out for one more. There was something about the night that was special. Maybe it was an off-shoot of cabin fever. Maybe that's why St. Patrick's Day is so popular.

Adversity Isn't a Hurdle, It's a Building Block

I can't thank Meredith Hall enough for this column.

Hall is a writer and professor at UNH. Her book, *Without a Map,* was featured in Oprah's magazine and is a national best-seller. If you haven't read it, it's amazing.

It's a memoir about Hall's struggles of teen pregnancy in Hampton, New Hampshire, during the 1960's and having to give up her child.

Reading it gave me a sense that you can write about a horrific event in your life and not sound bitter.

I met Meredith Hall at a writing conference and talked to her. Eventually, I e-mailed her a copy of this column, thanking her for her writing and her method. She responded with this:

> *You are a fine writer. I hope that you find more and more readers. They will be lucky to discover your clear and energetic prose, and your intelligence--of both mind and heart.*

Hands down, it is the finest compliment I've ever received from a fellow writer. I hold her in high regard, and when I doubt myself, I think about things like this. I still hold this piece up as an example of my best work.

McCune's Manchester
April 30th, 2009

I'm in my yard, pounding makeshift stakes for a makeshift fence into a makeshift garden when a picture of my father comes into my mind. He's tilling the garden. Carefully, he walks to the side of the old rear-tine tiller, as the old earth meets the air, soft and ready for the seeds he will plant later that afternoon. I'm about six or seven in this mental image and I don't realize how poor we are.

I'm thinking about those days more and more now. I've been out of full time employment, its benefits, and my old co-workers since February. The ground was hard and cold and covered in snow then. Now, it's soft and wet and renewed with the hopes of Spring.

The stakes I'm pounding are new, but the fence is most certainly not. In fact, I would say it's at least ten years old, maybe more. I scavenged it while driving by a house on Cilley Road a few weeks back. A year ago, I might not have been so bold as to knock on the door and ask "what's the story with the fence panels?" But this is different. This year we widened the garden, and added another, then another. There is more riding on these gardens now. It's a way to save money, it's a promise to my family that we will see through this economic storm no matter how long it lasts.

I think of this as I pound in the stakes for the fence. I think of my father and his tiller and myself and my tiller and my son watching me. The work is clean, and the pain I feel in my muscles and joints reminds me of the good thing I'm doing. I think of my family history, how my ancestors endured so much. How my great-grandmother faced the Great Depression alone, a divorced mother of two kids, de-barking downed trees for loggers in the Wisconsin woods so her children could eat.

I think of her son, my grandfather, who told me

about how they moved from place to place when he was a child. Missouri, Oklahoma, Oregon, and Wyoming, where his father would work as a foreman on the infamous Teapot Dome oil line. I think of how his uncle being a baker helped them through as he lived on fried flour and water.

Later, my great-grandmother and her two children would finally stop their furious moving pace. They settled in Wisconsin, closer to her mother. My grandfather and father, perhaps as a psychological result of this constant motion, still live in that same county, two miles apart.

I've finally figured out what my father taught me about perseverance. Adversity isn't a hurdle, it's a building block in our lives. To be a "McCune" is to persevere. I'm humbled by what my ancestors endured and their tired old lessons won't be forgotten. They say that those who forget the past are condemned to repeat it. Some of the steps I'm taking are repetitions of the steps my great-grandmother has taken, or those my father has taken. I don't see this redundancy as a curse or condemnation, but as a way to honor them.

My great-grandmother was a bulky woman. She was a trooper and a fighter. I spent the better part of my childhood visits with her being very afraid of her presence. She was loud, but would talk in hushed tones around my great aunt. The two of them would talk like friends gossiping about things unknown to me.

My great-grandmother would remarry, with the stigma of a 1920's divorce apparently lifted, she started over. She was generally happy, smiling as she handed us a jar of apple-butter whenever we were leaving. There was something still that struck me about her when we saw her. I now know this for what it was; stubbornness. In that sense, she was an old mule, letting family secrets die with her. Perhaps those secrets were too painful in her world to talk about. I can't help but wonder what missing parts of my history are out there.

I've heard stories of what other people are going through as we all face this economy together. Most of the stories are about situations far worse than ours. We have a house, we have some money coming in, we have our health and now we have a beautiful garden or three. And for all of that I'm thankful.

As I pound the last stake for my crooked, rickety fence, I noticed my two year old staring at me in wonder. He's learning the lessons I've learned and he's taking mental notes. Someday he will hear about his great-great-grandmother. He'll hear stories about a time that will seem foreign to him, and names of people he'll never see. We'll go over worn photographs of ancient faces. He won't know what it all means until one day when he's standing in his own garden with his own son thinking about the garden his father poured his heart into during the summers of his youth. Maybe then it will dawn on him what it all means: we are all going to be okay.

Memorable Birthdays

I have to hand it to the Goffstown Fire Department, they did an amazing thing with this.

I suppose they had no idea they would end up in the newspaper for it, but they did. Even on a budget of next-to-nothing, we were able to make a birthday party happen. Go figure.

McCune's Manchester
June 4th, 2009

A six-year-old's birthday party can be a delicate thing.

It's a tender age. The transition is beginning from Kindergarten to grade school, and they are certainly becoming socially aware. Kids can be "cool" for a certain pair of shoes, or a t-shirt, or even a haircut. This attitude seems too soon to me, but I can't deny its existence.

So when my son turned six this week, I knew we had to be careful.

We also had to be cheap, considering our budget has been put on a diet.

My wife and I were sitting on a bench in the mall a few months ago, wondering aloud what we were going to do for his impending birthday. A woman sitting next to us chimed in.

"I don't mean to eaves drop," she said. "But, I have an idea for your party. Take him to a fire station."

"That sounds interesting," my wife responded.

"We did that for our son a few years ago. He loved it," she said. I sat for a moment, running the idea through my head.

"And it's free," she said. Well, that sealed it.

We contacted our closest fire station, which happened to be off Mast Road in Pinardville. They seemed a little on their heels at first, but soon, I could tell the firemen liked the idea as well.

"What would you do?" one of the firemen asked.

"I was thinking just a tour, whatever you might do for kids at a school."

"I think we can do that," he said with a smile.

The kids had an absolute blast, and I think the firefighters had an even better time. My son, and his four guests climbed around the firetruck, posed for pictures with a fireman's heavy jacket and helmet and even saw a fire-hose in action. At the end, they were treated to sticker badges as "honorary firemen and women."

My son took it all in. He and his friends had permanent smiles the whole time, and hardly noticed that it started to rain.

We thanked the men on duty and headed back to our house for cake, ice cream, and the most important thing for any child's party; the presents.

I tell you, we could have went any number of ways for his party. We could have went to an arcade, or game room. We could have sprung for a dozen pizzas, but none of it would have had a lasting impression.

The next day, when I picked my son up from school, a few of the party-goers came over, wearing their honorary badges and still grinning from the party. I'm not sure pizza would have had the same effect.

I want to caution you, if you try this, make sure the treat the firemen with respect. They are on duty and have to be ready to go. We were told this a few times along the way. There was always the possibility they would get a call and have to move out. After all, they have a job to do, and one that's more important than showing off their cool trucks for kids.

Having a birthday party in a down economy can still be done. It just takes a little creativity, some ingenuity, and a little help from an anonymous person at the mall.

The next day, when my son woke up, the first thing he asked was if we could go back to the fire station. Maybe when one of his friends has a birthday.

There's a Long Road to Travel on Health Care

I had a difficult time writing this column. Here's the rub: the trip became very political and I didn't like it. I struggled with what I should say about it, and in the end, kept it light-hearted.

Here's the real situation; I felt a little used. The trip started great. I was interview on WMUR, I boarded the bus, we took off and away we went.

The next morning, we had a town-hall style meeting with our reps. I was supposed to speak.

They handed me a card with certain talking points on it. I ignored it and said what I wanted to say instead. Then, at the rally, I started seeing shirts with the Acorn logo on them. They were the group criticized during the presidential election for being shady and overzealous. When I asked one of our group leaders about the connection, they shrugged it off as a parallel rally.

My suspicions were growing.

Then, I followed a group as they loudly marched. They were violently shoving their signs and yelling. I ceased being a participant and started just observing.

They marched to the Ronald Regan Republican building. I was disgusted with their behavior. They were swearing, throwing things and generally carrying on like fools. I've never talked much about my personal politics, but it's worth mentioning here that I'm fiercely Independent. Politics aside, the behavior of the people at this "rally" was sad.

Men in bow ties on the third story sat and laughed at the people below. The entire scene was just a big political stereotype. I walked back, alone to the bus station, bellied up to the bar and ordered a beer while I waited to leave.

What did I expect? I went to a rally in Washington D.C. and expected it to not get political? In the end, I felt good about the experience. I learned so much about the process and what really happens, that I feel it was worthwhile. But I also learned a very valuable lesson; be careful of the motives of others, you never know when you might be used as a political pawn.

McCune's Manchester
July 2nd, 2009

My feelings about Politics are like my feelings about the Red Sox. It's important, it's a part of me, and I can't go a day without talking about it. But, I also feel I'm closer to becoming a relief pitcher for the Sox than I am to becoming a part of the political process.

So, when I boarded a bus with 40 strangers, heading overnight to Washington, it was a foreign moment to me.

I ended up making it to the bullpen at the Senate.

More than 100 Granite Staters took three separate buses last Thursday as part of a national rally for Health Care for America Now and other groups.

I was along for the ride to tell my story. When I lost

my day job, now five long months ago, I lost my health care benefits. My two boys are now covered under two separate insurers, while my wife has insurance through her work and I go without.

Part of me felt like a spoiled brat. I was riding a bus with people in varying degrees of health, all trying to grab some sleep on a long ride on a bus with severely unbalanced tires. The constant rattling kept most of us up all night as we pushed towards the Capitol.

My story is unfortunately typical right now, and because of this, I felt the need to represent my situation in Washington. Still, there were others that are worse off, and some were making the same trip.

There was one couple, a husband and wife from New Hampshire who's story got to me. He had to quit his job to take care of his ailing wife, who is suffering from Multiple Sclerosis, forcing her into a wheel chair. His situation forces him to provide for his wife's health full-time. The agonizing choice he makes is to be dirt-poor, but still married.

He was told he could easily file for divorce, and reap the benefits of being a health care provider. Instead, he remains lovingly by his wife's side. He probably eats more Ramen noodles than he would care for, but he remains true to his promise as a husband. For richer or poorer, in sickness and in health.

Well, I felt like a heel. Here I was, packing a pillow and blanket, and watching movies on my portable device during my trip. My only discomfort was the small space on the bus. Yet, on another bus, this couple suffered the same trip, with much less comfort and much more dire possibility at the end.

I had my moment last Thursday, where I felt knee deep in the political process. Senator Shaheen listened to the group that traveled down during a town hall meeting. She heard my story, and asked that I send a copy of my speech to her. It felt good to be in the thick of it.

Still, for all the good feelings, I had some reservations. The town hall meeting was supposed to be with all our representatives. I understood why Judd Gregg wasn't there, this wasn't his crowd. He has made his feelings on health care clear, and they are contrary to the group's ideas. I don't agree with him, but at least I understood. For the other two, Carol Shea-Porter and Paul Hodes, I was left scratching my head.

I wasn't alone in wondering why they didn't show up. Both support the group, and both sent down aides to talk in their place. I understand the life of a congressman or woman is probably hectic. For all I know, they were in a meeting. But Shaheen made it happen. And if it were me, and a group of people traveled a rickety bus overnight to talk to me, I would make the time.

There were moments during the rally, where things were becoming too political for an issue that should be void of politics. New York Senator Charles Rangel spoke at the rally, twice comparing the days events to Martin Luther King's march on Washington all those years ago. It was as bold a statement as it was silly. Even if the Senate and the House convened for a special ten-minute session to pass all proposals, it wouldn't be in the same league as the civil rights movement. I was embarrassed to listen any more.

Later, the Granite State group boarded the bus and nosed it towards Manchester. We were tired, some were sick, and most felt pretty good.

A week ago, I became a part of that distant political process. I made a trip for a cause I feel passion for. To put it in baseball terms, it felt like suiting up for the Red Sox. Maybe we're closer to a public health insurance option than I am to working the 7th inning at Fenway.

Unemployed and Time on His Hands

I still say this is a valid idea, even with its inherent flaws. Bureaucracy is never an answer, but I still think something like this would really work, and I haven't heard anything to suggest otherwise.

McCune's Manchester
July 30th, 2009

Being unemployed, I have a lot of time to think. Some might say too much time.

Lately, I've been feeling like a waste. There is such a thing as male pride. Sure, the whole image of the man being the "bread winner" and "putting meat on the table" may be somewhat old fashioned and even archaic, it still exists and it's still valid.

Week in and week out, I sit on my laptop, applying for positions, receiving rejections e-mails and hoping that the right job will come along.

The Federal stimulus has given me a boost in pay on my unemployment checks, but I don't see how it possibly stimulates any sort of growth. It certainly doesn't really help.

I don't feel guilty collecting unemployment. I've earned that money. Over the years, I've slowly been stashing it away and now I'm able to use it. But drawing unemployment basically excludes me from taking a majority of the jobs out there.

Let me share with you how it works. Basically, I'm getting the maximum benefit, around $400 a week.

That chimes in around $10 an hour for a 40 hour week. Not great, but I could be doing worse. In fact, with two children, taking a job paying $10 an hour job, I would lose money. Daycare expenses are through the roof, and staying at home with them is a much cheaper alternative.

In fact, day care is going to cost at least $125 a week. That means I have to make about $13 an hour just to cover day care.

I'm not complaining about being a dad, nor do I think the system should pay more, but I do see another problem that can be solved because of the Army of the Unemployed.

Right now, the people who have jobs are overworked. They've had to pick up the slack for the employees let go because of job cuts. Municipalities are feeling this crunch too.

Take a look at any random sidewalk in the city. Right now, most are covered with weeds. When are municipalities supposed to find the time to clean these areas right now? Moreover, because of budget cuts, it's hard to even justify the manpower for these type of things.

Here's my idea; make me do it. Seriously. In exchange for stretching out how long I can collect unemployment, let's say I donate five hours a week to the city. I can easily find someone to watch the kids for that amount of time and not feel like a burden. The city looks better, doesn't have to pay for the extra help, and can allow their workers to get to more important things. It eases the burden on the city, gives a bit of a break to the taxpayer, makes the area look better and gives me a bit of self-worth and accomplishment. Maybe I'm not putting steak on the table, but at least I could feel like I helped.

There is probably some big problem with doing a plan like this that I can't foresee. Perhaps it would create some giant bureaucratic mess that would be impossible to unsnarl. I don't know, it's just an idea.

The idea doesn't have to end with just weeding of course. I'm sure there are a host of other jobs able-bodied people like myself can do with little risk for the city or to myself. Obviously, I shouldn't start driving a snowplow or anything like that. I just want to feel useful.

There are a slew of city-based non-profits that could benefit from such an idea, it certainly can extend beyond weeds. These non-profits can enjoy the influx of new volunteers and the workers can pad their resumes. I called the New Hampshire Unemployment Security Office and they said we are one of the states where you can volunteer and still collect unemployment, so long as it doesn't interfere with your ability to find and secure a full-time job. In some states, you don't even get that option.

I told you I have too much time on my hands.

Coughing Without Insurance

There is not exaggeration here. I honestly thought I was going to die. That was by far the worst I've ever felt. My regular doctor told me he now thinks I had pneumonia or severe bronchitis. This had restricted my airways so much I could hardly breath.

It took six months of regular inhaler use to recover from this, and a part of me still worries it might come back again.

Still, this scenario, and the decisions I made because of it, are the clearest personal example I can give about why the whole health care industry needs to be turned on its head. Start over from the ground up.

I'm thankful I lived through this, and I have to say a big thank you to the doctors that took care of me. There were a couple of others, namely the worker who questioned why I was in a wheelchair, who I'm still quite angry with.

None of that matters now, I'm here. I made it, and now I have health insurance....in a broken system.

McCune's Manchester
September 17th, 2009

I thought I was going to die.

I know when people say that, they usually don't really mean it, but I actually thought I might be a goner.

It started a few weeks ago. This year, I had been lucky with allergies. I watched everyone around me suffer during allergy season. Normally, I'm right along with them. But I went through the spring and most of the summer without any allergy attacks whatsoever.

When they hit, I was almost in disbelief. So much so,

that I neglected to take any medication for them.

By Monday of last week, the coughing and wheezing forced me to make an appointment with my doctor.

This was not my first option. I would rather tough it out, and being without health insurance certainly colors that decision. Reluctantly, I went. They said it was probably bronchitis, and wrote me a prescription for an inhaler and a series of antibiotics.

It turned into an all-day ordeal, dragging my son with me to the doctor's office, the pharmacy and finally, back home to rest and wrap my head around my new series of drugs that I was suddenly taking.

At first, everything seemed to be helping.

At about 7:30 that night, it hit again. I coughed until I nearly passed out, clutching my chest as I fell to my knees. My boys watched in obvious horror, as I comforted them between coughs, telling them I was going to be okay. My wife was working late all week, so the chore of putting the boys to bed, making lunches and preparing for the next day rested entirely on my shoulder.

By 8:30, everything had calmed down. I felt I had made it through the worst of it. I was wrong.

All week, at nearly the same time, I would have another attack. By Saturday night, I was a mess. I had only gotten a fraction of the sleep I needed. My eyes were bloodshot, I was pouring in sweat, and I was taking my inhaler once an hour. The coughing had completely taken over by 9:00pm. At 9:30, we called Catholic Medical Center's Ask a Nurse hot line. They suggested I come in to the Emergency Room.

Having a sleeping baby with no one else available to

watch him, and not wanting to bring him into an Emergency Room environment, we made the decision that I would have to drive myself, and my wife would stay home with the baby. We can't afford an ambulance, and I couldn't afford to wait for anyone else.

I've never been admitted to an Emergency Room. I hope I never have to again. I answered the same series of questions three times between labored breathes and hacking coughs. My appearance certainly gave everyone else a reason to worry. Here I was, in my sweat pants and a t-shirt, absolutely drenched in sweat, whooping the worst cough I've ever heard. Everyone stared, including some of the staff. One worker asked why I was in a wheelchair. I didn't have an answer for that, and just looked at her while I coughed. I could read everyone's eyes, workers and patients alike, as they stared at me in horror. Their eyes said "Swine-Flu". Even a priest gave be the same concerned look. I hoped I wouldn't need to talk with him later.

I felt lost, trying desperately to control my breathing, and feeling terrible for the nurses that drew the short straw and took care of the big, sweaty-coughy guy. Two hours, and a nebulizer treatment later, I was in my hospital bed fighting off sleep between visits from the doctor and scenes from The Bourne Identity, playing on the television.

Luckily, I found out about a program that the hospital, in fact, most hospitals offer to people like me, who find themselves in need of emergency care and little means to pay for it. I'm not even sure what the final bills will all total, but at least I know I might be offered some reprieve.

Every decision during this ordeal was tempered with dollar signs in my head. Initially, I didn't make an appointment because it would cost money. Then, I neglected to call my doctor for fear of another hospital visit. In the end, that became the catalyst to only cost me more money at the ER. If I had any insurance, I would have taken a ride int the ambulance. Instead, I had a very harrowing three mile trip that I luckily was able to make it through.

They wrote me a new prescription and I walked next door to fill it up. I drove home at midnight, breathing and smiling. I still feel lucky to be alive.

During Search for Work, He Also Found Himself

This was the culmination of all of these events. From February to October of 2009, I was an active job seeker. My future was uncertain, but my vision was never clouded, and I never gave up.

In the end, I really enjoyed the summer taking care of my boys. I was able to spend so much time with them. I'll cherish that summer forever. I had my moments, but overall, I kept my cool and just loved my kids.

I've vowed to never walk into an unemployment office again. If I ever go through this again, I hope that things have changed; the system, the job market, and myself.

I became a better person through this process and that is what matters...that, and I have a job.

McCune's Manchester
October 1st, 2009

I'm now gainfully employed.

Last week, I accepted a job as the Assistant Media Services Coordinator for the Town of Merrimack. Big title. Basically, I will work for one of the coolest public access channels in the state, if not New England.

When I found out I got the job, there was an enormous weight lifted off my shoulders. The past eight months I've been unemployed, have been an excruciating process, to say the least.

In that time, I've felt worry, doubt, fear, happiness, depression, anger, caution, frustration, excitement, relief, disgust, hope, and finally peace. I've come to understand things about myself that I never knew. I found that I can be an awesome gardener. I figured out that there is nothing stopping me from getting what I want, and that sometimes the only limiting factor in my own goals is myself.

I've always been a creative person, that will help me in my new position, and it helped me during unemployment. As soon as it was clear that I was going to be collecting unemployment for a long period of time, we put a plan into action at our house. We bought a second-hand roto-tiller for the garden. We expanded the garden, knowing that we might need to rely on it during the lean times. At first the idea sounded scary and paranoid to me, but after using the tiller, I felt comfort in knowing that I accomplished something.

We cut coupons, we scoured the grocery store ads, and stocked up when there was a sale on bread or chicken or any common staple. We bought a used freezer. Right now, that thing is filled with the sales of the summer and gallons of tomato sauce from the bounty of our garden.

We cut out expenses. We cut back everywhere we could and somehow, there were times when it seemed we had more money than before I was laid off. Of course, there were times when I wondered if we were going to make it.

But we did. In the process of looking for work, it seems I found myself. I learned to trust myself, and to cherish the time I had this summer with my two boys. I had to trust that things were going to be okay, but understand that nothing would change if I didn't make it. The opportunities that are out there for people on unemployment are few, but they are there. In the end, I didn't settle for a job that I would hate. Instead, I waited and found the one that would be right.

Humans are funny creatures. We toil and struggle sometimes for little result and few rewards. But above all, we are built to last. We can be stubbornly prideful creatures, sometimes to our own detriment. But in the end, those things can strengthen who we are.

There is something to be said about the notion of male pride. There were moments that I didn't even want my kids looking at me. It's a very subtle and complex emotion, but it is cut from such a simple place. Being a man means having a job. Being a father and a husband means providing for your family. To put meat on the table is such a silly, overused cliche, but it makes sense to me now.

Last week, I went down to the unemployment office in Manchester, to straighten out some wrinkles in my unemployment status. This had nothing to do with the new job, and everything to do with the new online system, which is a mess.

Sitting in the waiting area, I vowed it would be the last time I would ever have to be there. The process is painful, but necessary. There is no shame in collecting unemployment. It isn't "welfare", as one crass ex-coworker told me. It's a system you buy into from the moment you start working. For me, that started two weeks after my 14th birthday, when I started working at a grocery store. Since then, I've earned the right to collect unemployment.

For those still collecting unemployment, I can only offer the advice that worked for me. Plan for the long-haul. Find yourself. Don't stress too much, and don't take out your frustrations on those around you. Above all, know that things will work out. They always do.

I will never forget those months I spent wondering what was next. Someday, I'll look back and smile, knowing that was when I re-discovered myself, my self worth, and learned that I was going to make it.

There is Much to be Thankful For

This column is largely similar to the last selection, with one important difference: I thank you, the reader.

I owe all of my success to you. This book, my column, the turns I've taken in the last few years are all because you keep reading.

I feel so incredibly blessed with this column and the support I've received because of it. All I can do is thank you from the bottom of my heart.

So while this may be a little redundant, I wanted to put this column in this book as a dedication to anyone who has read my column and taken away anything, good or bad, from it. Any emotion you feel, I feel... and if that is all I get out of this, then it is a huge reward to me.

McCune's Manchester
November 26th, 2009

I'm sitting here, Tuesday morning, at 10:30, and I'm still in my pajamas, staring at a mostly blank screen wondering what exactly that I'm going to write.

This column comes out on Thanksgiving Day. You're reading it now, snuggling up to the television for the Thanksgiving Day Parade, in preparation to the onslaught of turkey and football that the day brings.

I'm sitting here, wondering just exactly how I put into words what I'm thankful for this year. I'm thankful, mainly for this column. This column has allowed me the avenue to express myself. I feel like when I'm most successful with this column, is when I'm reflecting what is going on in this city. I'm an average guy with average thoughts, trying to do something above average. Some people call that the American Dream.

2009 has had its ups and downs for me, for Manchester, and probably yourself. It hasn't been easy, but at the same time, I feel a sense of relief. Part of that is because of my recent full-time employment.

Moreover, it's knowing that I've sifted through this mess and found out who I am.

This past year has been a roller-coaster. My wife and I spent the final weekend of January celebrating our wedding with a truncated honeymoon in Maine. I came back to work in February to find that no job was waiting for me.

The rest of February was spent worrying about what was next. That wonder and worry consumed me and my young family in that time. It took me a long time to settle in and figure out what was really happening.

By the time I started collecting unemployment checks, the worry was settling away. I looked for signs that I was on the right track, and four months into my forced sabbatical, I won a national award for this column. It was justification.

It was a defining moment for this year for me. I was collecting unemployment, with worry consuming me and I received this little nudge that told me I was doing the right thing.

I'm thankful now, that I have full, regular employment. Beyond that, I'm thankful for knowing that if the day shall come again that I am unemployed, I am more than capable of plowing through.

I hope what makes my story unique is that it really isn't unique at all. Many of you have gone through similar moments of doubt and worry. It is how we get through those moments that shapes us into who we really are.

This city has been dealing with those same moments of doubt and worry, yet it still keeps moving forward. I hope that is what defines Manchester.

All those things that happened to me, happened to a lot of people in this city. I guess today's column is selfish, but it came after a lot of reflection. It's a reflection I hope you take in on yourself this

Thanksgiving.

So eat your turkey and pumpkin pie, watch some football, and snooze a little on the couch today while you think about what you are thankful for.

I have my family, I have my health, and I have you, the reader. Those are things I'm thankful for.

Thank you.

Made in the USA
Monee, IL
07 July 2026